How Not *to Get Rich*

⋆ HOW *NOT* TO ⋆

GET RICH

⸻ ❧ ⸻

The Financial Misadventures of

MARK TWAIN

Alan Pell Crawford

HOUGHTON MIFFLIN HARCOURT

BOSTON   NEW YORK

2017

For information about permission to reproduce selections from this book,
write to trade.permissions@hmhco.com or to Permissions,
Houghton Mifflin Harcourt Publishing Company,
3 Park Avenue, 19th Floor, New York, New York 10016.

hmhco.com

Library of Congress Cataloging-in-Publication Data is available.
ISBN 978-0-544-83646-4

Book design by Victoria Hartman

Printed in the United States of America
DOC 10 9 8 7 6 5 4 3 2 1

To Albert Epshteyn

Contents

Author's Note

Just a quick warning.

Readers hoping for a full-dress biography of Mark Twain might want to move on. A number of excellent Twain biographies are both easily obtained and well worth reading. Ron Powers, Fred Kaplan, Justin Kaplan, Jerome Loving, and Hamlin Hill, among others, have written books on Twain that I've read, enjoyed, referred to, and even quoted in *How Not to Get Rich*. Most recently, Richard Zacks, in his estimable book *Chasing the Last Laugh,* offers a rich and absorbing look at Twain's later years, as Michael Shelden has also done in *Mark Twain: Man in White.*

How Not to Get Rich, by contrast, attempts to offer a financial biography of Twain—as a kind of angel investor, speculator, inventor, and what used to be called "plunger." Here readers will see a different side of this remarkable man—a man far less concerned with his literary efforts than with his investments, including numerous seemingly ridiculous inventions and contraptions on which he squandered millions of his own dollars.

A few are Twain's own inventions, but he didn't discriminate. Twain wasted a lot of money on others' bad ideas too.

"Mark Twain was no ordinary genius," a great nephew of his once recalled. Twain, he said, "tried to be an Edison as well as a Shakespeare, and a few other great men besides." This book attempts no facile explanation for why Twain was so obsessed with making a great fortune. There's a place for a good psychobiography of Mark Twain, but this isn't it.

Twain's financial story is enough for one book. Readers who make it to the end of *How* Not *to Get Rich* will probably agree with that same great nephew's assessment: Twain "was a devil to do business with — but you can't help loving the man."

Another thing: Because *How* Not *to Get Rich* is about Twain's business life, it's about money. That means there are dollar figures throughout. Readers will want to know what the amounts referred to from 1877, for example, would be worth today. There are any number of methods for converting dollar figures from the past to their equivalents during other times, including our own. Making these determinations is always a challenge for historians, and no completely satisfactory method exists.

Throughout this book, I've relied on calculations provided by www.in2013dollars.com, which uses a historical study of inflation rates conducted by Robert Sahr, a political science professor at Oregon State University. Despite its name, the site allows for conversions to 2016 values. I've also checked many of these figures on a comparable site called MeasuringWorth .com, which relies on U.S. government statistics but only allows for comparison to 2015 values.

The results are rough estimates of what a given sum might be worth in our time. When a range of possible equivalents is offered, I've gone with the lowest and, I assume, the most conservative estimate. In 1877, for example, a maid in Twain's Hartford house was paid about $150 a year. Plug in those numbers and we learn that she would be making $3,300 in our time. The cook was paid $240 a year—or $4,400 now. Whether that salary was earned or not probably depends on what Twain thought of the cooking. That of course could vary from meal to meal as well as from year to year, and there's no way to quantify a man's moods, especially Twain's.

ALAN PELL CRAWFORD
SPRING 2017

How Not *to Get Rich*

1

"Whatever I Touch Turns to Gold"

Like most of us, Mark Twain hated writing checks to other people. But there were times when he happily paid out large sums. Issuing a check for $200,000 drawn on the United States Bank of New York on February 27, 1886, for example, made him almost giddy. The check was made out to Julia Dent Grant, the widow of Ulysses S. Grant. The former president of the United States and commanding general of the Union Army had died of cancer the summer before, just after completing his remembrances of the Civil War. That payment represented the first profits from sales of volume one of the *Personal Memoirs of Ulysses S. Grant,* published only a few months earlier by Charles L. Webster & Company, a startup publishing house that Twain had established two years before. He had installed a nephew, Charles "Charley" Webster, as its business manager. Webster got his name on the letterhead and a salary, but that's about all he got out of the position, besides aggravation. Twain made all the business and financial decisions, except when he didn't feel like it.

Twain would have been pleased to have published Grant's memoir even if it had not broken all American publishing records for sheer profitability. Just landing the contract had required Twain to persuade General Grant to break a handshake deal with another publisher. The other publisher had offered Grant a 10 percent royalty. Twain countered by offering a royalty share unheard of then or since: 75 percent. The other publisher offered no advance against royalties. Twain said he would pay $25,000 upfront.

This was a bold gamble—some might say a reckless investment—but it paid off. At that time, the $200,000 royalty check to Grant's widow was the largest ever paid by an American publisher. In the months to come, Webster & Company wrote additional royalty checks to Grant's family, bringing its earnings to $450,000, which again broke publishing records. Twain himself pocketed $200,000 for Grant's memoirs. In our own time, that's about $11 million for Grant's widow and $4.8 million for Twain.

This sounds like a lot of money—and it was. In 1886, a coal miner made $1.50 per day and paid $6 per month to rent a house for his wife and five children. The family's annual food bill was $80, a pound of butter cost 35 cents and a dozen eggs, 40 cents. For the urban sophisticate, a man's suit cost $4.85, a piano could be bought for $125, and a three-bedroom apartment in Manhattan rented for $80 a month.

BY THE AGE OF FIFTY, Mark Twain had achieved something he had dreamed of and worked for his entire life: He was rich. Raised in genteel poverty in small towns in Missouri (when Missouri was still the West), Twain as a grown man had rubbed elbows with the greatest business tycoons of the time. As the author of *The Innocents Abroad, Roughing It, Life on the Mis-*

sissippi, *The Adventures of Tom Sawyer,* and *The Adventures of Huckleberry Finn,* he had seen the world, or much of it. Russian princes and English lords fawned over him. Hundreds of thousands of people bought his books and lined up to hear him speak. With his earnings—and his wife's inheritance—he had built a startlingly opulent, twenty-five-room mansion in high-toned Hartford, Connecticut. Justin Kaplan, the author of *Mr. Clemens and Mark Twain,* called the house "part steamboat, part medieval stronghold, and part cuckoo clock."

And now, as head of his own publishing firm, making money for other authors, he felt like a great philanthropist. He could see himself as one of the true benefactors of the era. And it was an era he had named when he chose the title of one of his own bestsellers: *The Gilded Age.*

MARK TWAIN WAS born Samuel Langhorne Clemens on November 30, 1835. For the purposes of this book, he is Mark Twain, not Samuel Clemens—and that's final. Twain's place of birth was Florida, Missouri, which contained 100 people at that time. By being born there, he recalled,

> I increased the population by 1 percent. It is more than many of the best men in history could have done for a town. It may not be modest in me to refer to this but it is true. There is no record of a person doing as much—not even Shakespeare. But I did it for Florida and it shows that I could have done it for any place—even London, I suppose.

In the interest of scholarly thoroughness, it should also be pointed out that Twain never did much else for his hometown. Today, Twain tourists go instead to Hannibal, where he grew up and they can feast on Roughin' It Burgers at the Mark Twain Dinette and Family Restaurant. As of the 2000 census, there were only nine people living in Florida, Missouri. By 2010, the village was officially uninhabited, though this is unfair. The person who answers the phone at the Mark Twain Birthplace State Historic Site, a quarter of a mile from Florida, says the town's population in July 2017 was in fact four. The site is worth visiting, in any case. A modern musuem there protects the actual cabin where Twain was born.

Perhaps more significant than *where* Twain was born is *when*. In *Outliers,* Malcolm Gladwell discovered that of the seventy-five richest people in human history, fourteen were Americans born within nine years of one another. John D. Rockefeller, the richest ever, was born in 1839. Andrew Carnegie (#2) was born in 1835, and so on down the line, through Jay Gould (#33) and J. P. Morgan (#57) and all the others. What's going on here? Gladwell asks.

Then he tells us:

> The answer becomes obvious, if you think about it. In the 1860s and 1870s, the American economy went through perhaps the greatest transformation in its history. This was when the railroads were being built and Wall Street emerged. It was when industrial manufacturing started in earnest. It was when all the rules by which the traditional economy had functioned were broken and remade.

What Gladwell's list of rich men and their birth dates says is "it really matters how old you were when that transformation happened." And Twain and Rockefeller, et al., were all in their twenties and thirties when it took place. (So, of course, were untold millions of people who were born just when Gladwell recommends but died poor anyway.)

The sociologist C. Wright Mills observed much the same phenomenon decades before Gladwell and came to this conclusion: "The best time during the history of the United States for the poor boy ambitious for high business success to have been born was around the year 1835." And Twain wasn't born *"around* the year 1835," but *during* it—a strategic decision of the utmost significance, suggesting an alert and eager business mind operating even in utero.

UNFORTUNATELY, TWAIN WAS not so astute in his choice of parents. His father was John Marshall Clemens, an upright and humorless man, a Virginian by birth, and, by occupation, a failed storekeeper, failed boardinghouse operator, and failed lawyer. These Clemenses claimed descent from Geoffrey Clement, who in 1649 was one of the judges who sentenced Charles I to die by beheading. Twain's mother, the former Jane Lampton of Kentucky, was a pious though lighthearted woman whose family also talked of an illustrious British ancestry. Though American by birth, one of Jane Lampton Clemens's nephews called himself the rightful Earl of Durham.

If there was gentility in Mark Twain's background, it was of the shabby kind, at least by the time he came along. Neither of his parents brought "an over-surplus of property" into the marriage; his mother's dowry consisted of "two or three Negroes but nothing else." They were a slaveholding family, with a household servant or two. What the servants actually did is hard to figure. After John Clemens died in 1847, the family lived above a drugstore. Twain's mother cooked for the druggist's family and did their laundry. "Money is better than poverty," Woody Allen once said, "if only for financial reasons." Twain knew this from childhood.

The Clemens family lived in Tennessee before moving to Missouri, and it was there that their dubious patriarch made a momentous financial decision. John Clemens would become a land speculator. Resigned to the likelihood that he would never earn much money, he determined to provide for his family after his death by acquiring vast holdings in real estate. From 1826 through 1841, he bought twenty tracts in rural Fentress County, Tennessee, totaling between 35,000 and 75,000 acres. John Clemens claimed they owned 100,000 acres. Historians disagree on the precise number, which isn't surprising since the family itself never seemed sure. He spent about $400 for the land—maybe $11,000 today—and died telling his survivors to hang on to the property until the time was right. Resist the temptation to sell it to the first bidder. If they would only be patient, they would be rich, as any fool could see.

"Whatever befalls me, my heirs are secure," John Clemens said. "I shall not live to see those acres turn to silver and gold but my children will." Besides the mineral wealth under the ground, there were "grazing lands, corn lands, wheat lands, potato lands, there are all species of timber—there is everything on this great tract of land that can make land valuable."

These were boom times in America when Mark Twain's father bought the Tennessee land. This period of economic expansion that was unleashed by laissez-faire capitalism, in the words of John Maynard Keynes, constituted "the magnificent episode of the nineteenth century." The federal government offered for sale 28 million acres of public lands, leading to enthusiastic real estate speculation. More than a quarter of the population now lived west of the Appalachians. The way people and goods moved was changing. By 1840, locomotives owned by 300 railroad companies were rattling along 3,300 miles of iron rails. Steamboats, which plied the waters of the Great Lakes, would soon connect north and south on the Mississippi.

Alexis de Tocqueville marveled at "the phenomenal release of initiative and energy" in the men and women of John Clemens's time. A historian with the wonderful name Garet Garrett called it "the breathless generation." Henry Adams said "the continent lay before [Americans] like an uncovered ore-bed." Technological advances stimulated economic development on scores of fronts. There was Cyrus McCormick's reaper, John Deere's steel plow, Samuel Morse's telegraph, and Josephine Houghton's hand-cranked dishwashing machine. (Josephine Houghton was a Shelbyville, Illinois, housewife inducted into the National Inventors Hall of Fame in 2006. Unfortunately, this was too late to do her much good, considering that she died in 1913.)

The same iron industry that turned out thousands of miles of rails was producing everyday items vital to settling the West —knives, axes, and plows. It also turned out thousands of revolvers, useful for cowboys shooting each other and for settlers trying to persuade Indians to abandon tribal lands that these newcomers wished to inhabit. This population boom, John Clemens said, "will henceforth increase faster than ever. My children will see the day that immigration will push its way to Fentress County, Tennessee, and then, with 100,000 acres of excellent land in their hands, they will become fabulously wealthy."

This tantalizing prospect of great wealth bedeviled Mark Twain for much of his life. It spurred him on as few other things did. All truly ambitious people can point to something like this in their lives, and they can be resentful of it but grateful, too.

"We were always going to be rich—next year," Twain recalled. "It's good to begin life poor; it is good to begin life rich—these are wholesome, but to begin it poor and *prospectively* rich! The man who has not experienced it cannot imagine the curse of it!"

And few with such a curse upon them ever appreciate how motivating it can be.

MARK TWAIN'S FAMILY was poor but possessed lively imaginations. They strained to burst out of their limited financial circumstances. Twain's father put his hope in the Tennessee land, but that was not all. He also fancied himself an inventor, trying to produce a perpetual-motion machine. Twain's older brother Orion (pronounced *ORE-ee-on*) spent long hours at work on a flying machine.

Although intelligent and hard-working, Orion "inherited his father's aptitude for failure," according to R. Kent Rasmussen, a Twain scholar. When their father died, Orion became the de facto head of the family, responsible for the Tennessee real estate investment and providing for the family day-to-day. To that end, he owned and edited the *Hannibal Western Union* newspaper, where Mark Twain was employed as a "printer's devil," setting type—if "employed" is the right word since he worked without pay.

Twain had other jobs in Hannibal and seems to have been fired from all of them. He worked in a grocery store, in a tannery, and in a blacksmith shop. He worked at an apothecary, though "my prescriptions were unlucky, and we appeared to sell more stomach pumps than soda water." He worked in a bookstore, but that didn't work out either, because "customers bothered me so much I could not read with any comfort." Eventually Orion took him on in the newspaper's print shop. In time,

Twain did get paid, and it was in the *Hannibal Western Union* that his first literary efforts were published.

Only in retrospect does the appearance of Twain's first writings seem like a historic occasion. He never viewed them as such, because he was not aware, then or for years to come, of any great literary calling. Self-styled "thought leaders" who say great success depends on finding one's passion in life and pursuing it like a honey badger with an unrealistic agenda will find little support in these pages. Twain's passion wasn't to work in a print shop, pilot riverboats, write for newspapers, or even — as he would do in his twenties — prospect out West for gold and silver. Twain's goal was to make money and then make even more money. Writing books was just a means to an end, and in 1886, when he wrote that check for $200,000 to General Grant's widow, he was well on his way to realizing his dream.

And now that he was amassing his fortune, he could accomplish even more. Because he was a successful publisher, he could stop writing altogether and make money off other authors' books. He could invest in other businesses as well. He could be what we'd call an "angel investor" or venture capitalist. He could even turn his attention to his own inventions. He could do what his luckless father and brother had tried to do with their inventions but lacked the aptitude, connections, and financial wherewithal to succeed.

Twain felt there was almost nothing he could not accomplish, as he admitted to a friend just months before his first payments to Grant's widow. "I am frightened by the proportions of my prosperity," he said. "It seems to me that whatever I touch turns to gold."

2

"That Splendid Enterprise"

Like many boys full of spirit and imagination, Mark Twain was never comfortable in the classroom. Albert Bigelow Paine, his authorized biographer, said Twain "detested school as he detested nothing else on earth," and scholars seem to agree that his formal education ended when he was twelve. Upon his father's death in 1847, Twain's mother took their mischievous son into the room where the body lay and implored him to be a better boy. "I will promise anything," he said, "if you won't make me go to school." Twain assured her he would hereafter be industrious and responsible, and forswear alcohol (but not tobacco). Twain's mother consented. He never darkened a schoolhouse door again, except in later life when he took a daughter off to college or agreed to make an appearance or give a lecture.

But Twain was an avid reader. In 1856, when he was not yet twenty, he was working as a typesetter in his older brother Orion Clemens's new print shop, the Ben Franklin Book and Job Office. This was in Keokuk, Iowa, where there wasn't much to do but read. Biographer Ron Powers describes Keokuk as a "hotbed of rest." It was there that Twain happened onto William Herndon's *Exploration of the Valley of the Amazon: 1851–1852.*

This book made a slam-bang impression. Lieutenant Herndon was a great explorer who, while serving in the U.S. Navy, led an expedition from the headwaters of the Amazon to its mouth, over mountains and through jungles as yet unknown except to the tribes that lived there. Herndon's 4,000-mile trek was a magnificent adventure, Twain recalled years later, "through the heart of an enchanted land, a land wastefully rich in tropical wonders, a romantic land where all the birds and flowers and animals were of the museum varieties, and where the alligator and the crocodile and the monkey seemed as much at home as if they were in the Zoo."

But what caught Twain's fancy was not the fauna but the flora — one particular specimen of flora and its effect on the Inca Indians of the Andes. Herndon said these Indians were "silent and patient" in their seemingly endless labors in the silver mines because they enjoyed a ready supply of the *Erythroxylon* coca plant, now known as the source of cocaine. Chewing coca evidently elevated the workers' mood and suppressed their appetite. It enabled them to labor tirelessly without complaint, precisely as would be wished by the industrialists who soon made their appearance in North and South America.

As long as they had "coca enough to chew," Herndon observed, the Incas would do "an extraordinary quantity of work." They would take a break every morning, chew a little more coca, and then go right back to work. "It has made me, with my tropical habit of life, shiver to see these fellows puddling with their naked legs a mass of mud and quicksilver in water at the temperature of 38 degrees Fahrenheit," Herndon wrote. It bothered him to watch these men working as hard as they did, but as long as they had coca leaves to chew on, it didn't seem to bother them. Morale might not have been high, but "corporate culture" wasn't an issue one way or the other.

Twain was even more impressed than Herndon with the secret of maintaining such a dependable workforce, which was not then to be found in team-building exercises or the incentives of stock options and bonuses. Twain thought the coca plant possessed "miraculous powers." It was "so nourishing and so strength-giving" that Incas working the mines "require no other sustenance."

Of course, Twain did not understand coca's addictive and otherwise harmful properties. Not even the American drug companies recognized its dangers when they first began to market it decades later. In the early days, coca was used to flavor Coca-Cola—hence the name. Cocaine's so-called recreational use did not become widespread until the 1970s. The blame for this can be cast widely, but no one, so far, has accused young Mark Twain of anything untoward, and they should not. By recognizing the financial possibilities of the coca leaf, Twain was simply ahead of his time.

WE UNDERSTAND A GREAT DEAL that people in Twain's time did not. One of the great discoveries of our own age is that to succeed in business, you have to have what James Collins and Jerry Porras, in their 1994 classic *Built to Last: Successful Habits of Visionary Companies,* called a Big Hairy Audacious Goal, or BHAG. If you or your organization don't have a BHAG, you are probably doomed to fail, no matter how smart you are or how hard you work or even how great your mission statement might be. A BHAG, they say, is a "huge daunting challenge" that might be absurdly bold, but is at the same time clear, compelling, and energizing; also, it has a readily identifiable goal, even if it takes decades to reach it.

Collins and Porras didn't invent BHAGs; they just identified them and gave them a name. In fact, BHAGs date back thousands of years, "at least to Moses," as Collins said in an interview. Henry Ford had one, as did Tom Watson of IBM. And it's significant that a true BHAG looks "more audacious to *outsiders* than to insiders." Insiders don't "see their audacity as taunting the gods." It never occurs to true visionaries that they can't do what they set out to do.

Mark Twain's BHAG was to corner the world's cocaine trade. "I was fired with a longing to ascend the Amazon," he recalled. Specifically, he felt "a longing to open up a trade in coca with all the world. During months I dreamed that dream, and tried to conjure ways to get to Para [Brazil's seaport] and spring that splendid enterprise upon an unsuspecting planet." To that end, he assembled an organization—also key to achieving your BHAG, as Collins and Porras advise. Twain talked up the enterprise and recruited at least two eager associates. One was Joseph Martin, a Keokuk physician and lecturer in chemistry and toxicology at the Iowa Medical College—an astute move on Twain's part, since Twain knew next to nothing about either subject. The other was a man named Ward, supposedly a businessman in the neighborhood, but that is about all anyone has been able to figure out.

Twain, Martin, and Ward "agreed that no more shall be admitted into our company." Although Orion had expressed interest in kicking in startup money, Twain didn't even want his older brother included. Shortly before he set off for the Amazon, Twain told their younger brother Henry Clemens how skeptical he was of Orion's reliability and motives. He and Ward had determined to start to Brazil, if possible, in *six weeks* from now, in order to look carefully into matters there . . . and report to Dr. Martin in time for him to follow on the first of March. We propose going *via* New York. Now, between you and I and the fence you must say nothing about this to Orion, for he thinks that Ward is to go clear through alone, and that I am to stop at New York or New Orleans until he reports. But that don't suit me. My confidence in human nature does not extend quite that far. I won't depend upon Ward's judgment, or anybody else — I want to see with my own eyes, and form my own opinion. But you know what Orion is. When he gets a notion into his head, and more especially if it is an erroneous one, the Devil can't get it out again . . . Ma knows my determination but *even she* counsels me to keep it from Orion.

Although Orion "talks grandly about furnishing me with fifty or a hundred dollars in six weeks," Twain wrote, "I am not such an ass as to think he will retain the same opinion such an eternity of time — in all probability he will be *entirely* out of the notion by that time." Orion probably just wanted Twain "to take all the hell out [of] pioneering in a foreign land, and then when everything was placed on a firm basis, and beyond all risk, he could follow himself."

So, on April 15, 1857, Twain set off for New Orleans on the *Paul Jones,* with thirty dollars to his name. By now, Martin and Ward had — for unexplained reasons — lost interest in the project. This left Twain, as CEO, on his own. With stops along the way, the *Paul Jones* reached New Orleans on April 26, by which time Twain was so low on funds as to be suspected of vagrancy.

In New Orleans, Twain "inquired about ships leaving for

Para and discovered there weren't any and learned that there probably wouldn't be any during that century." He also found out that no ship had ever left New Orleans for Para. This was bad news. Twain needed to think about what it meant. "I reflected," he would recall. "A policeman came and asked me what I was doing, and I told him. He made me move on, and said if he caught me reflecting in the public street again, he would run me in."

Twain biographer Albert Bigelow Paine says it never occurred to Twain "that it would be difficult to get to the Amazon and still more difficult to ascend the river. It was his nature to see results with a dazzling largeness" that sometimes blinded him to unpleasant realities. Or, as Twain himself admitted much later in life, beyond getting to New Orleans and from there to Brazil and making his fortune, "This was all the thought I had given to the subject. I never was great in matters of detail."

On the streets of the City That Care Forgot, Twain's grand scheme to corner the cocaine market died. But for a mere quirk in maritime transport, the man we know as the creator of Tom Sawyer and Huckleberry Finn would never have had to go to the trouble of writing those books at all. Literature was Twain's side hustle, after all, and had there actually been ships traveling from New Orleans to Brazil and back, he might be known today as the El Chapo out of Keokuk or as a proto–Pablo Escobar.

But to his great credit, Twain seems to have lost little sleep over this early setback, which is a characteristic of all great business leaders. They are resilient. They let the past go, acknowledge their own shortcomings, and take reversals of fortune in stride. They see new opportunities and grab them. Twain said,

By temperament, I was the kind of person that DOES things. Does them, and reflects afterward. So I started for the Amazon without reflecting and without asking any questions. That was more than fifty years ago. In all that time my temperament has not changed, even by a shade. I have been punished many and many a time, and bitterly, for doing things and reflecting afterward, but these tortures have been of no value to me; I still do the thing commanded by Circumstance and Temperament, and reflect afterward. Always violently. When I am reflecting on these occasions, even deaf persons can hear me think.

Realizing he needed a Plan B, Twain left New Orleans on April 30, just four days after his arrival. And even before his boat pulled out from the docks, being smart, resourceful, and quick on his feet, Twain had found his new calling.

3

"Do You Gamble?"

The pilot of the *Paul Jones* was Horace Bixby. This veteran of the Mississippi was at the wheel on the return trip from New Orleans when he turned to see a young man with a mop of red hair. Bixby noticed that the stranger spoke in a peculiar, drawling manner. People in that part of the country called it "pulling" one's words.

After introducing himself, the young man said he wanted to be a pilot too and asked if Bixby would train him. Pilots in those days could keep such an apprentice, or "cub." The cub could travel with the steamer, at no cost to himself or to the pilot.

There was something oddly endearing about this visitor, and Bixby was intrigued. Keeping his eyes on the river, he asked, "What makes you pull your words that way?"

"You'll have to ask my mother," Twain said. "She pulls hers too."

What followed was a job interview, or what passed for one in less officious times.

"Do you drink?" Bixby asked.

"No."

"Do you gamble?"

"No."

"Do you swear?"

"Not for amusement; only under pressure."

"Do you chew?"

"No, Sir, never," Twain answered. "But I *must smoke.*"

Twain had been a smoker since he was nine—"a private one during the first two years, but a public one after that—that is to say, after my father's death." Smoking wasn't considered so objectionable then, except by exceedingly upright parents. It was not considered a problem, even in the workplace.

"Did you ever do any steering?"

"I have steered everything on the river but a steamboat, I guess."

"Very well," Bixby said, stepping to the side. "Take the wheel and see what you can do with a steamboat. Keep her as she is—toward that cottonwood snag."

Twain must have done well enough, for the two soon entered into negotiations—or as Roger Fisher and William Ury of the Harvard Negotiation Project would have us say, they were *Getting to Yes.* For any negotiation to succeed, each party must want or need something from the other, as all the experts on negotiating skills tell us. What Twain needed was money. With his dreams of a world trade in coca leaves dashed, he also needed a career. And while Twain might not have known it at the time, there was something Bixby wanted from Twain, or from almost anybody, for that matter. Bixby had a sore foot. This made it painful for him to stand at the wheel for hours on end, maneuvering a 300-foot steamboat around tangles of fallen trees, as well as past islands that seemed to appear overnight, and steering the boat to ramshackle docks along the riverbank—half of the time when it was almost pitch dark and difficult to see.

Bixby could use some relief at the wheel, but that assistance would have to come from someone who was confident, quick on his feet, and dependable enough to count on in the long days and nights ahead. Such a person would also have to be sufficiently intelligent to learn the river, which meant committing to memory the ever-changing Mississippi's maddening idiosyncrasies.

The youngster who stood before Bixby in the pilothouse seemed to fit the bill. Still, there remained the matter of money. Bixby said he would charge $500 to take Twain on. The training would take two years. After that, the cub could get his license and go out on his own. The pay would be handsome. But during his apprenticeship, he would receive no compensation, except for room and board, courtesy of the steamship company.

"I haven't got five hundred dollars in money," Twain said. But, remembering the supposedly great fortune his father had left, he made a counterproposal. "I've got a lot of Tennessee land worth twenty-five cents an acre; I'll give you two thousand acres of that."

Bixby had no interest in "unimproved real estate." The country had a surplus of it. You could see endless stretches of it up and down the river. There was almost nothing but empty land whichever way you looked.

"Well, then," Twain said. "I'll give you one hundred dollars cash"—which of course he didn't have—"and the rest when I earn it."

The *Paul Jones* was headed for St. Louis for repairs, which proved fortuitous. That is where Twain's sister Pamela lived. Pamela (pronounced *Pam-EE-lia*) had married a prosperous merchant named William Moffett. Twain borrowed the $100 down payment from Moffett and paid Bixby. And when the *Colonel Crossman*—Bixby's next piloting assignment—pulled away from the docks, Twain was in the pilothouse with him, studying the river and filling the first of several notebooks with what Bixby taught him.

As for Bixby's sore foot, history is silent. But he spent the rest of his life piloting riverboats and was still working until 1912, when, at the age of eighty-six, he died.

THIS BEGAN THAT part of Twain's life with which he is most closely associated, next to being an author. This at least is the period he romanticized, which is understandable. Being a steamboat pilot was a glamorous calling, especially for boys raised in drowsy river towns where the passing of these floating palaces was a momentous event. As a boy in Hannibal, Missouri, Twain and his friends had only one lasting ambition in life.

> When a circus came and went, it left us all burning to become clowns; the first negro minstrel show that ever came to our section left us all suffering to try that kind of life; now and then we had a hope that, if we lived and were good, God would permit us to be pirates. These ambitions faded out, each in its turn, but the ambition to be a steamboat man always remained.

These boys were raised in the golden age of the steamboat, which, like many golden ages, was short-lived. In those days, pilots—not captains—commanded the ships they steered. The sons of doctors were happy to become lowly clerks on the river. Liquor dealers' sons became bartenders in the ships' saloons. But the pilot had "the grandest position of all," Twain wrote in his autobiography. "The pilot, even in those days of trivial wages, had a princely salary—from a hundred and fifty to two hundred and fifty dollars a month, with no board to pay."

But for the two years of his apprenticeship, Twain struggled. When he wasn't accompanying Bixby on one of his runs, Twain took odd jobs. Once, to make ends meet, he was a night watchman, keeping an eye on cargo piled up on the New Orleans levee.

Twain was twenty-three when, on April 9, 1859, he finally obtained his license. He made his first run as a fully accredited pilot on the *Alfred T. Lacey,* enjoying "an income equal to that then earned by the Vice President of the United States." When Twain steered the *City of Memphis,* "the largest boat in the trade," he boasted that he could put away $100 a month, and this was after sending money to support his mother. When he went to pay his dues to the Western Boatman's Benevolent Association, he told brother Orion, he liked "to let the d—d rascals get a glimpse of a hundred dollar bill peeping out from amongst notes of smaller dimensions, whose faces I do *not* exhibit! You will despise this egotism, but I tell you there is a 'stern joy' in it."

WE KNOW THE ERA of the riverboat as a golden age mostly because Twain told us it was. And it was a spectacular, if somewhat sketchy, business. By the time Twain took the wheel, a thousand such vessels plied the Mississippi, Missouri, and Ohio Rivers, carrying more cargo than all the country's oceangoing ships put together. The railroads were only getting started and, at that time, could hardly compete for sheer glamour with those "moving mountains of light and flame," as one account calls them. They were ornate and gaudy, imposing to look at, fun to party on—and extremely dangerous.

Owners of these riverboats made far more money hauling cargo than entertaining pleasure-seekers (including gamblers and prostitutes) in their saloons. Some carried a thousand tons of cargo at a time, which weighed them down so much they virtually skimmed along the river bottom. The lifespan of these riverboats was less than five years. Many had their hulls ripped open, sometimes by striking the wreck of another steamboat that had met its own disastrous fate and sunk. The boats belched smoke and sparks, and those that did not run aground were likely to catch fire and explode. The year after Bixby and Twain were its pilots, the *Colonel Crossman* itself blew up.

Twain clearly enjoyed the work as well as the pay, and a popular image of him to this day is at the wheel of a riverboat, his unruly hair billowing out from beneath a pilot's cap. But this is misleading. In fact, Twain was a pilot for only about four years—and this part of his life came to a close at the same time the steamboat's role as a major force in American commerce had begun to wane. The movement of goods by water was about to experience what we would call a "disruption." The Civil War shut down Southern shipping, and in the postwar years, the government subsidized the railroads with cash and land grants. Besides, the railroads moved goods faster, more economically, and with greater safety than did the steamers.

Our business culture celebrates disruption—as long as it is confined to industries other than our own. "Disruptive innovation," as it's known today, can be disastrous for people whose living depends on the industry whose old ways of doing things is disrupted. In this case, that meant anyone who made his living on the river. But disruption can be a great motivator, as it was for Twain. The turning point, for him as well as for the riverboats, was the Civil War. He was in New Orleans in April 1861, when President Lincoln announced a blockade of the

South, including the Mississippi, and Twain was suddenly out of work. While Bixby stayed on throughout the war, piloting an ironclad Union gunboat, Twain, a Southern sympathizer in his early years, had other ideas.

These ideas were clarified in May 1861, when he was a passenger on the *Nebraska,* heading north. The *Nebraska,* piloted by his friend Zeb Leavenworth, had secured clearance to pass through the blockade at Memphis. Unfortunately, an artillery unit from a Union outpost just south of St. Louis seems not to have known this fact.

Twain was in the pilothouse with Leavenworth when a warning shot from the Union soldiers crashed into the *Nebraska*'s smokestack, shattering glass and reducing wooden ornamentation to splinters.

"Good Lord, Almighty!" Leavenworth cried out. "What do they mean by that?"

"I guess they want us to wait a minute, Zeb," Twain said.

Then, with seemingly superhuman aplomb, Twain took the wheel himself and turned the boat around. Eventually allowed to push on, the *Nebraska* reached St. Louis. By this time, Twain's momentary bravado (we have only his account of it) appears to have evaporated. He never talked about what he did next. For that, we have to rely on his sister Pamela Moffett's account.

4

"I Had to Seek Another Livelihood"

Once the *Nebraska* reached St. Louis, Twain fled to his sister Pamela's house. There he hid out, Pamela said, obsessed with the fear that government agents would arrest him. He was convinced they would force him, at gunpoint, to pilot Union ships and shoot him at "the least sign of a false move."

So, as soon as the opportunity presented itself, Twain hightailed it back to Hannibal. Although Missouri did not secede from the Union, it was a slaveholding state, full of Southern sympathizers. Like most Americans, north and south, Twain thought the war would be over in a matter of months, and maybe sooner. Always eager for adventure, he served for a few weeks in the Marion Rangers, a volunteer militia unit supposedly dedicated to protecting their native Marion County from invading hordes of Union marauders. There were fourteen members of this outfit, for which the overused word "ragtag" seems especially fitting, and Twain was elected second lieutenant. The Marion Rangers had no uniforms. Their only weapons were whatever was at hand. Mostly, they camped out in the woods.

Whenever federal troops appeared in the general vicinity, the Marion Rangers would find reasons to camp farther away. Within days, Twain resigned on the grounds that he was "incapacitated by fatigue" from nonstop retreating. But his time with the Marion Rangers was educational, if nothing else. Twain "learned more about retreating," he said, "than the man that invented retreating."

So Twain waited for the war to end. He assumed that when it did, and shipping on the Mississippi resumed, he would go back to piloting—as a civilian. "I supposed—and hoped— that I was going to follow the river the rest of my days, and die at the wheel when my mission was ended," he said. But when the war dragged on for four more years, and "commerce was suspended, my occupation was gone. I had to seek another livelihood."

TWAIN'S RESPONSE TO the war was, arguably, both sensible and businesslike. He took measures to avoid getting killed or dying of disease, and in that he was far more successful than some 700,000 of his countrymen. What he did after resigning from the Marion Rangers was to move out West, more than a thousand miles from Antietam, Gettysburg, and Appomattox.

Of course, not getting killed was easier for some Americans than for others. If you were rich (Twain, recall, was only "prospectively rich") you could hire a substitute to serve in your stead. John D. Rockefeller did this. So did Andrew Carnegie, J. P. Morgan, Jay Gould, and Philip Armour the meatpacker. Finding a replacement recruit was perfectly legal and respectable—if you had enough money.

Those who thought of themselves as the best people paid for

replacements (or their brokers did); the richer you were, the more likely you were to do so. Once you didn't have to fight in the war yourself, you could turn your attention to making money from the war, as some of these shrewd men did. They included John Wanamaker and Clement Studebaker, as well as the Brooks brothers, who made uniforms. Carnegie added to his wealth by speculating in rail and bridge construction, all the while serving as assistant to the assistant secretary of war in charge of military transport. Some, including Elisha Brooks, one of *those* Brooks brothers, palmed off their shoddy goods on the armies, which outfitted unfortunate soldiers with cardboard shoes, flimsy clothes, and guns that didn't fire. Twain, by contrast, harmed no one when he avoided military service. He cost the country far less, in fact, than did bounty jumpers and profiteers. And when Twain left for the West, he was actually doing government work, of a sort.

Twain's brother Orion Clemens had campaigned for Abraham Lincoln in 1860, and in early 1861 he was appointed secretary to the Nevada Territory (pop. 6,857). This was "a not negligible position, easily the most prestigious that Orion would ever have," with a salary of $1,800 a year. When the government studiously ignored Orion's appeals for an advance to pay his way west, Twain himself agreed to foot the bills. In return, Orion made his brother his secretary—the secretary to the secretary, that is. That's how the government did things back then. Today, of course, we are more efficient.

The brothers set off by steam and stage for Nevada on July 11, 1861, taking two days in Salt Lake City so that Twain could gawk at polygamists. On August 14, they arrived in Carson City, the capital of the Nevada Territory. Just two years earlier, the Comstock Lode of gold and silver had been discovered only 200 miles away, at Mount Davidson, giving rise to riches that came and went with astonishing speed. There wasn't much for the secretary to the secretary to do, so mostly Twain lazed about, except when he went sightseeing.

In September he visited Lake Tahoe, or, as it was known at that time, Lake Bigler. About fifteen miles west of Carson City, the lake astonished him with its clear, deep waters and surrounding pine forests. Its unspoiled beauty practically intoxicated him, as it would millions of visitors in years to come. There were no casinos there, of course, or ski lodges and vacation homes, though these would come sooner than one might think. Just three years after Twain's visit, Tahoe City would be founded as a resort for residents of Virginia City, more populous then than Carson City and situated about forty miles northeast of the lake. For now, though, the lakefront was an ideal campsite. Three months of camp life on Lake Tahoe, Twain said, "would restore an Egyptian mummy to his pristine vigor, and give him an appetite like an alligator. I do not mean the oldest and driest mummies, of course, but the fresher ones." The air in that high altitude was "pure and fine, bracing and delicious."

But Twain also saw commercial possibilities in those forests. As the son of a man who had bought thousands of acres back in Tennessee, Twain had been raised with an awareness of the profits to be had from undeveloped real estate. The land around Lake Bigler, of course, would have to be despoiled for its riches to be realized. Despoiling natural resources was never a goal of any such enterprise, of course—only a consequence or byproduct. By the time Twain laid eyes on the forests around the lake, logging was already supplying timbers to shore up the Comstock mines. The cost of entry in the timber business was negligible. Squatters could do pretty much what they wanted; possession was at least 90 percent of the law. You had to mark your claim, which evidently could be done simply by fencing off the trees you wished to cut down. The fence could take almost any form. It need not be sturdy. You also had to put up some kind of structure to serve as a house. It needn't be sturdy, either.

Twain and a friend named John D. Kinney built such a house by the lake that fall. Because they enjoyed sleeping under the stars, they never actually slept in it. Inhabiting their shack "never occurred to us," Twain said. They did not ask too much of their flimsy structure, which "was built to hold the ground, and that was enough. We did not wish to strain it."

One night, after rowing from another camp with a fresh supply of provisions, Twain began to fix dinner. At about 7 p.m., he took bread, bacon, and a coffee pot, put them all under a tree, built a sturdy fire, and went back to the boat for his frying pan. The next thing he knew Kinney was shouting something at him. He turned to see his fire "galloping all over the premises" and Kinney racing through the flames to get back to the water's edge.

A good six miles from anyone who might be able to help, the two entrepreneurs stood, as in a daze, watching flames consume the forest. Because the ground was a carpet of dry pine needles, the fire "touched them off as if they were gunpowder," Twain wrote in *Roughing It*. In this memoir of his days out West, he claimed to have enjoyed the spectacle.

> It was wonderful to see with what fierce speed the tall sheet of flame traveled! My coffee-pot was gone, and everything with it. In a minute and a half the fire seized upon a dense growth of dry manzanita chaparral six or eight feet high, and then the roaring and popping and crackling was something terrific.

The intense heat sent them scurrying back to their boat, and there they stayed—and watched.

> Within half an hour all before us was a tossing, blinding tempest of flame! It went surging up adjacent ridges— surmounted them and disappeared in the canyons beyond—burst into view upon higher and farther ridges, presently—shed a grander illumination abroad, and dove again—flamed out again, directly, higher and still higher up the mountain-side—threw out skirmishing parties of fire here and there, and sent them trailing their crimson spirals away among remote ramparts and ribs and gorges, till as far as the eye could reach the lofty mountain fronts were webbing as it were with a tangled network of red lava streams.

Every so often, Twain or Kinney would remove his pipe from his mouth and exclaim, "Superb, Magnificent! Beautiful!"

The fire raged for four hours, and by 11 p.m., "the conflagration had traveled beyond our range of vision, and the darkness stole down upon the landscape again." As for supper, the bread was cooked, the bacon fried, "but we did not go to see. We were homeless wanderers again, and without any property. Our fence was gone, our house burned down; no insurance. Our pine forest was well scorched, the dead trees all burned up, and our broad acres of manzanita swept away. Our blankets were on our usual sand-bed, however, and so we lay down and went to sleep."

The next morning, they roused themselves and gaped again at the surrounding desolation. If they did anything more about the damage they caused, there is no evidence of it, and no expectation that they should have. Innocent of any highfalutin' notions about "sustainability," they had simply stood by and watched in wonderment as the wildfire they touched off with such unforgiveable irresponsibility pumped carbon dioxide into the atmosphere, contributing to manmade climate change. (Readers who find the scientific evidence for manmade climate change lacking may express their concerns directly to the publisher.)

Twain and Kinney did notice, when they saw each other that morning, that they "looked like lava men . . . covered as we were with ashes, and begrimed with smoke." Then they just shrugged their shoulders, packed up what was left of their belongings, and headed back to Carson City. There, one hopes, they bathed.

5

"All That Glitters"

After successfully burning down a forest, Twain returned to Carson City, where he was soon "smitten with the silver fever." This was predictable, as an older and wiser Twain would later realize: "I would have been more or less than human if I had not gone mad like the rest," he would say in his own defense. Day after day, he'd seen wagonloads of solid silver bricks rolling down the street, and "such sights as that gave substance to the wild talk about me. I succumbed and grew as frenzied as the rest." The mountains were said to be "literally bursting with gold and silver," and Twain believed it.

The rich veins of the Comstock Lode had lured prospectors by the thousands just as the California Gold Rush began to peter out. At its peak, around 1863, the market value of the silver produced by mines in the Comstock was $40 million. Among those who struck it rich in those raw, windswept ranges was George Hearst, the father of William Randolph Hearst. In the winter of 1859 alone, the elder Hearst mined thirty-eight tons of silver.

It was at the age of twenty-six that Twain decided that silver "was the road to fortune" and set off on that dusty trail with characteristic self-assurance. Over the next four years, from 1861 to 1865, he made several determined forays into the mountains. All the while, he watched as others made their fortunes, some of them literally overnight. Some were foolhardy enough to pocket more money than they'd had in their lives, then drink it all away, realize they were broke again, and have to start all over.

A quick study, Twain began to speak knowingly of veins, ledges, leads, yields, claims, riffles, screenings, assayers, and assessments, peppering his conversation (and letters home) with other oddments of mining jargon. There was no reason he would not strike it rich in the unspoiled Nevada Territory, he told his mother. Nevada

> is fabulously rich in gold, silver, copper, lead, coal, iron, quicksilver, marble, granite, chalk, plaster of Paris, (gypsum), thieves, murderers, desperadoes, ladies, children, lawyers, Christians, Indians, Chinamen, Spaniards, gamblers, sharpers, coyote's [*sic*] (pronounced ki-yo-ties), poets, preachers, and jackass rabbits.

It was also a forbidding landscape. The birds that fly over it "carry their own provisions with them."

How could a young man of ambition and brains not succeed in this wide-open environment?

TWAIN BEGAN AS a mere prospector, hauling picks, shovels, and other tools into the mountains. He was not at first sure, however, why he and his friends would need this burdensome equipment. From the due diligence that he had conducted, it seemed the precious metals would be practically begging for a good home.

> I confess, with shame, that I expected to find masses of silver lying all about the ground. I expected to see it glittering in the sun on the mountain summits. I said nothing about this, for some instinct told me that I might possibly have an exaggerated idea about it, and so if I betrayed my thought I might bring derision on myself. Yet I was perfectly satisfied in my own mind as I could be of anything, that I was going to gather up, in a day or two, or at furthest a week or two, silver enough to make me satisfactorily wealthy . . .

One day, he came back to camp too excited by what he had discovered in a shallow riverbed to contain himself. Although he had been content until now with "vulgar silver," he had stumbled onto something he thought was far more valuable. In his eagerness, he gave in to the temptation to show off the shimmering yellow samples he had gathered and sought an expert's opinion of its worth. He handed the samples to a sixty-year-old prospecting partner and asked the man what he thought of the discovery.

"Think of it!" the old prospector responded. "Think of it? I think it is nothing but a lot of granite rubbish and nasty glittering mica that isn't worth ten cents an acre!"

From this episode, Twain drew a sharp lesson. "All that glitters is not gold," he said.

The prospector told Twain he could go further than that: "Nothing that glitters is gold."

Even getting to the places where prospectors thought they might find gold and silver turned out to be far more arduous than Twain imagined. On a frigid afternoon in December 1861, for instance, he and three other men loaded a wagon with 1,800 pounds of provisions and rolled out of Carson City for the Humboldt district, northeast of Lake Bigler.

The men were to ride in the wagon, which would be pulled by two horses. But when the horses proved old and feeble, the prospectors "found that it would be better if one or two of us got out and walked. It was an improvement. Next, we found that it would be better if a third man got out. That was an improvement also." At this point, Twain volunteered to drive, though he had no experience, "and many a man in such a position would have felt fairly excused from such a responsibility." But soon after he took the reins, "it was found that it would be a fine thing if the driver got out, and walked also."

Within an hour, the men further decided that they would take turns, two at a time, pushing the wagon through the sand, which left little for the horses to do "but keep out of the way." Shoving that wagon and those horses two hundred miles took fifteen days, if you counted the two days the men just sat around and smoked their pipes so the horses could rest. They could have made the trek in half the time, Twain figured, "if we had towed the horses behind the wagon, but we did not think of that until it was too late." Well-meaning strangers along the way suggested the prospectors might have made even better progress had they put the horses *in* the wagon.

ONCE THE PROSPECTORS got to a likely spot, their work didn't get any easier, nor did they become noticeably more efficient at working the ground. It took an hour to sink a shaft deep enough into the rocky soil to plant a charge and to blow a hole in the ground. One man would hold an iron drill while another slammed it with an eight-pound sledgehammer. After they had created a hole a couple of inches in diameter and two or three feet deep, they deposited gunpowder, covered it with rocks, dirt, and sand, lit the fuse, and ran for their lives. Once the blast went off and the rocks, dirt, and sand rained down, the prospectors would race back and, typically, find nothing more valuable than a small pile of quartz. "One week of this satisfied me," Twain said. "I resigned." The others resigned, too, and tried to think of different ways to meet the challenge. Instead of driving a shaft straight into the mountaintop, they decided they would dig a tunnel into the mountainside.

> So we went down the mountainside and worked a week; at the end of which time we had blasted a tunnel about deep enough to hide a hogshead in, and judged that about nine hundred feet more of it would reach the ledge. I resigned again, and the other boys held out only one day longer. We decided that a tunnel was not what we wanted. We wanted a ledge that was already "developed." There were none in the camp.

FOR ONE BRIEF SPELL in 1862, Twain was reduced to working as a laborer in a quartz mill. At the mill, quartz was pulverized and filtered and heated and rinsed and otherwise manipulated to dislodge whatever silver might be in it. This noisy and dirty work held no prospect whatever of making a man rich. All you did at the mill was help other men get rich. You processed other men's ores from six in the morning till darkness fell, with no breaks between. All day long, you were exposed to quicksilver, with the ever-present danger of mercury poisoning. The pay was $10 a week. This was a significant comeuppance, or "comedownance," for someone who saw himself, with every sunrise, as an incipient millionaire; it was a humiliating demotion for the son of a Tennessee real estate speculator whose heirs were "always going to be rich—next year."

There was always next year, and the next year after that. Back in Tennessee, Orion was supposed to be managing the sale of that land but he was getting nowhere. He had done some investigating and in the late 1850s determined that the family actually had title to only twenty-four tracts totaling just 30,000 acres. Even worse, the value of the acreage they owned was declining. A New York agency expressed interest in buying it for 10 cents an acre, and Twain's family back east was eager to get rid of at least half the property. "I think we had better take it," Pamela said. This was the best offer they had received. It wasn't much, but "every little we get now is of great importance to us." For some reason, the deal fell through, and Twain was becoming more and more impatient with the whole sorry business.

All the while he worked in the quartz mill, he worried about money. But this did not last long—the work, that is. In his first days on the job, he explained, he was put to shoveling sand onto a screen used to filter out any silver it might contain. But he never learned to swing the shovel properly. "All too often, the sand never made it to the screen at all, but went over my head and down my back." Twain found the work too hard, and he could well understand why the company "did not feel justified in paying me to shovel sand down my back."

Eventually, there came the inevitable parting of ways—a *mutual* parting of ways, Twain would insist in his autobiography. After a week, he went to his immediate supervisor. Twain explained that he "had never grown so attached to an occupation in so short a time, that nothing, it seemed to me, gave more scope to intellectual activity" as work at the mill. Even so, he "felt constrained to ask an increase of salary." The boss said he considered $10 a week "a good round sum," but how much did Twain want? About $400,000 a month, Twain claimed to have asked for—plus lodging. This "was about all I could reasonably ask, considering the hard times." Twain was ordered off the premises. Given how hard he'd worked, "I only regret that I did not ask him [for] seven hundred thousand," he wrote in *Roughing It*. But in his autobiography, Twain remembers the negotiations differently, though the outcome was the same: "I was discharged just at the moment I was going to resign."

Albert Bigelow Paine suggests that Twain worked in the mill with a larger purpose in mind than merely putting food on the table and tobacco in his pipe. "It was not entirely for the money that he undertook the laborious task of washing 'riffles' and 'screenings,'" Paine writes. "The money was welcome enough, no doubt, but the greater purpose was to learn refining." That way, when he owned mines and his own mills, he could "personally superintend the work."

This is persuasive as far as it goes. Learning a business from the factory floor, as it were, almost always makes sense. It is certainly easy to imagine Twain seeing himself as a superintendent of many things. No doubt superintending was what he thought he did best; many of us believe telling others what to do is our true core competency.

Paine is probably right, too, that Twain was coming to realize that, if he wished to succeed in a big way, being a mere prospector was not the best route. He and his friends found "the *real* secret of success in silver mining—which was, not to mine the silver ourselves by the sweat of our brows and the labor of our hands, but to *sell* the ledges to the dull slaves of toil and let them do the mining!"

He would have to become a speculator, too, and run the numerous businesses he planned to acquire with the earnings from his investments. As a speculator, he "bought and sold 'feet' and related interests like latter-day boys would deal in bubblegum baseball cards, and with about as much to show for it," Ron Powers writes in his Twain biography. Keeping meticulous records of his holdings, Twain became "conversant in mining pyrites, copper, selenite crystals, mica, water rights, even the effect of underground springs on rheumatism. He also grew familiar with the phrase 'played out.'"

Of course, speculating would not be easy, even when you were in the field yourself, staking claims to can't-miss opportunities. It wasn't even easy when you located a genuine bonanza. In the summer of 1862, the whole community was talking about a new claim, the so-called Wide West Mine, which the *Esmeralda Enterprise* reported as rich not only in silver but in gold. Crowds gathered, and free samples of the rich ore were given away to spark interest.

Recipients of these samples routinely took them back to their cabins and washed them to see for themselves if they were the real stuff. Cal Higbie, a kind of business associate with whom Twain shared a cabin, took his sample, rinsed it, ground it up, and examined it with a magnifying glass. One evening, he hid in the sagebrush and, when the workers had left the scene, he quietly slipped seventy-five feet down into the shaft and snooped around on his own. Then he climbed back to the surface, brushed himself off, and raced back to the cabin, "hot, red and ready to burst with smothered excitement," to tell Twain the good news: *"We are rich!"*

6

"Rich and Brimful of Vanity"

As the two men huddled in their cabin, Higbie told Twain about the discovery. The sample he had been given wasn't from the Wide West Mine at all, he said. It was from a vein that snaked its way parallel to the Wide West. It was a "blind lead," in mining jargon, meaning it was in no way visible from the surface and unlikely to be discovered except by sheer luck or, in Higbie's case, sheer snooping. Even better, a blind lead was anybody's for the taking. All you had to do was stake your claim to it, which would shut down operations on the existing mine. This would allow Twain and Higbie to get at the riches unmolested.

Twain, for once, was speechless. All his dreams were coming true. Once they secured this ore, he'd never need to work another day in his life. He'd never have to worry about that land back in Tennessee, or anything else. "I thought the very earth reeled under me," he wrote in *Roughing It*. "Doubt—conviction—doubt again—exultation—hope, amazement, belief, unbelief—every emotion imaginable swept in wild procession through my heart and brain, and I could not speak a word. After a moment or two of this mental fury," Twain asked Higbie to repeat himself.

"It's a blind lead!"

Twain responded. "Let's—let's burn the house—or kill somebody!" he exclaimed. "Let's get out somewhere where there's room to hurrah . . . It is a hundred times too good to be true!"

At ten on the night of June 20—remember that date—Twain and Higbie went to the recorder's office and entered their claim in the recorder's book. Historians disagree about exactly what securing their rights to the claim required, but judging from Section 11 of the Esmeralda Mining District, regulations were pretty minimal. You filed the paperwork. Then, to show you were serious, you had ten days to begin the hard labor of actually getting those minerals out of the ground. If you didn't start the work, your claim was forfeited, and at the stroke of midnight on the eleventh day, someone else could "jump" your claim.

After Twain and Higbie entered their claim and returned to their cabin, neither could sleep. Lying awake in their drafty, dirt-floor shack, they began to talk about how the riches they were about to reap would totally change their lives. As soon as the work was started, they agreed to leave Nevada, take a steamer out of California, and wait in the East for the silver to be mined and sold and their money to roll in. When they were flush, they'd move back to the West.

"Where are you going to live?" Higbie asked.

"San Francisco," Twain said.

Higbie said he would live there, too.

They'd agreed that Russian Hill would be the best place to build their houses but decided it might take too much climbing. They were sick of walking up and down hills. Then they remembered they would own carriages. So it would be Russian Hill, after all.

"What kind of a house are you going to build?" Twain asked.

"Three-story and an attic," Higbie said.

"But what *kind?*"

"Well, I don't hardly know. Brick, I suppose."

Twain sneered at brick. He had other ideas.

"Brownstone front—French plate glass—billiard-room off the dining-room—statuary and paintings—shrubbery and two-acre grass plat—greenhouse—iron dog on the front stoop —gray horses—landau, and a coachman . . ."

After a pause, Twain asked, "Cal, when are you going to Europe?"

"Well, I hadn't thought of that. When are you?"

"In the Spring."

"Going to be gone all summer?" Higbie asked.

"All summer! I shall remain there three years."

Higbie decided he would go too.

"What part of Europe shall you go to?"

"All parts," Twain said. "France, England, Germany—Spain, Italy, Switzerland, Syria, Greece, Palestine, Arabia, Persia, Egypt —all over everywhere."

Higbie thought for a moment and agreed it would be a "swell trip."

"We'll spend forty or fifty thousand dollars trying to make it one, anyway," Twain said.

Then, after a long pause, Twain added: "Higbie, we owe the

butcher six dollars, and he has been threatening to stop our—"

"Hang the butcher!"

"Amen."

THEY TALKED LIKE this until 3 a.m., then got up and played cribbage and, till sunrise, smoked their pipes. Twain continued to plan his European trip. He "managed to get it all laid out, as to route and length of time to be devoted to it—everything, with one exception—namely, whether to cross the desert from Cairo to Jerusalem per camel, or to go by sea to Beirut, and thence down through the country per caravan."

He also decided to write to friends back east, asking them to find a suitable home for his mother (which he would pay for himself, of course) and then sell his interest in the Tennessee land and donate the profits to the widows' and orphans' fund of the typographers' union.

But before he could start working the claim, he was suddenly called away to the sickbed of a friend nine miles out of town. Twain left a note in the cabin for Higbie explaining where he had gone.

Higbie, however, had decided to set off on his own in search of an even richer vein that everyone had begun to gossip about. Passing the cabin as he rode out of town, Higbie simply tossed a note for Twain through the window. Being in a hurry, he never went inside, where Twain's note lay.

Several days passed. Around midnight on June 30, Twain shambled back into camp, too exhausted to notice the crowd gathered around the Wide West, and went straight to the cabin. There, in the candlelight sat Higbie, staring in sullen disbelief at the note Twain had left him.

"Higbie, what—what is it?" Twain asked.

"We're ruined—we didn't do the work."

Higbie, it turned out, had never seen Twain's note because he had not gone back inside the cabin. Of course, Twain hadn't seen the note Higbie left for him because he hadn't been back either. Neither had done a thing about their claim, and it had been jumped. That's why the crowd had gathered at the shaft. Higbie had gone to see what the commotion was about, arriving ten minutes too late.

For an hour, "busy with vain and useless upbraidings," the two men tried to sort out what had gone wrong. Mostly they sat in silence. "A minute before, I was rich and brimful of vanity," Twain wrote in *Roughing It*. "I was a pauper now, and very meek." He tried to look on the bright side: "I can always have it to say that I was absolutely and unquestionably worth a million dollars, once, for ten days."

Now what can the astute business leader of today—the so-called lifelong learner—conclude from this episode, which Twain called "the most curious, I think, that had yet accented my slothful, valueless, heedless career"? Any consultant will tell you. The key to accomplishing anything in business (you see it in every PowerPoint presentation) is to *communicate, communicate, communicate.* Twain and Higbie had not even managed to *communicate,* or even *communicate, communicate,* much less *communicate, communicate, communicate.* That's the lesson here. There might be others, but that's the first one any of our self-styled "thought leaders" of today would spot.

THE PARTNERSHIP THAT found and lost the blind lead was not the only business organization in which Twain was involved in his mining days. He was also a partner in the Clemens Gold and Silver Mining Company (now defunct) with Orion as his partner. Theirs was a complicated relationship, personally and professionally.

"Send me $40 or $50—by mail—immediately," Twain wrote shortly after beginning his prospecting. "Don't buy *anything* while I am here—but save up money for me. Don't send any money home. I shall have your next quarter's salary spent before you get it, I think. I mean to make or break here within the next 2 or 3 months."

That was in April 1862. In May, he reported to Orion that the Clemens Company owned one-eighth of a new mine, and he wouldn't sell a share of it for any price "because I know it to contain our fortune." Before the summer was over, however, Twain began to worry—and was losing his patience with a brother who he felt was insufficiently supportive. The younger brother, he reminded Orion, was the mining expert and should be recognized as such.

> You have *promised* me that you would leave all mining matters, and everything involved in an outlay of money, in my hands. Now it may be a matter of no consequence at all to *you*, to keep your word with me, but I assure you *I* look upon it in a very different light. Indeed I fully expect you to deal as conscientiously with me as you would with any other man. Moreover, you know as I well as I do, that the very best course that you and I can pursue will be, to keep on good terms with each other—notwithstanding which fact, we shall certainly split inside of six months if you go on in this way ... Now Orion, I have given you a piece of my mind—you have it in full, and you deserved it—

Twain told Orion he would never look on their mother's face again, or their sister Pamela's, and that he would not get married "until I am a rich man—so that you can easily see that when you stand between me and my fortune (the one I shall make, as surely as Fate itself), you stand between me and home, friends and all I care for . . ."

WHEN THE CLEMENS COMPANY'S investments invariably went south, Twain struggled to hide his poverty.

During one eight-week stretch, Twain's sole occupation

> was avoiding acquaintances; for during that time I did not earn a penny, or buy an article of any kind, or pay my board. I became very adept at "slinking." I slunk from back street to back street, I slunk away from approaching faces that looked familiar. I slunk to my meals, ate them humbly and with a mute apology for every mouthful I robbed my generous land lady of, and [when] I slunk to my bed, I felt meaner and lowlier and more despicable than the worms.

Twain was a worm, perhaps, but a worm whose family had "vast" real estate holdings. There was always the land back in Tennessee. The possibility that his father's investment could someday pay off might have been what sustained him in his poverty—that and his indomitable spirit. There were times when Twain pretended to live like a prince. At one mining camp, he and a friend in similarly reduced circumstances would sneak about the other cabins, gathering empty champagne bottles and fruit tins. These they would pile outside their own shack, adding whenever possible the containers of the few delicacies they somehow managed to obtain for themselves. "In the course of a few weeks," a local newspaper reported, "the accumulation of cans that contained oysters, turkeys, jellies and other good things began to attract attention. Miners passing their cabin used to gaze upon the many cans and say, 'By Jove, those fellows live like fighting cocks!'"

7

"The Richest Place on Earth"

For anyone as resourceful and ingenious as Twain, there is always cause for hope. For several months in 1862 he had been contributing jokey letters to the *Territorial Enterprise*, a daily newspaper published in Virginia City, Nevada. In July of that year, the paper offered him a job. The pay was $25 a week—a considerable sum if you were broke, but almost an insult to someone who fully intended to be a multimillionaire and sometimes carried himself as if he already had achieved this lofty station. So, like the man who decides to work until something better comes along, Twain accepted the offer and set off on foot for Virginia City. It was there, on February 3, 1863, that for the first time one of his pieces appeared under the name "Mark Twain."

Virginia City was the Silicon Valley of the Comstock Lode, with the swagger of the Vegas Strip. Thrown up almost overnight, clinging to the eastern slope of Mount Davidson, Virginia City existed for the sole purpose of supporting the mining that went on not only around it but, literally, underneath it. Shafts and tunnels were dug 3,000 feet below the town; shacks, saloons, and storefronts shook and rumbled whenever miners set off their explosives. With a near-instant population of 25,000, almost all of them newcomers, Virginia City was known as the "richest place on earth," as Warren Hinckle says in his history of the town. "So fabulous were the fortunes produced and the manner of spending and squandering so superlative," he writes, "that it burns through the fog of historical memory as a Cinderella city, a real-life, uniquely American Camelot devoted to the questionable art of conspicuous consumption."

Naturally, Twain loved Virginia City, even if he sometimes felt constrained by having to work for wages. "I am very well satisfied here," he wrote to his mother. "They pay me six dollars a day, and I make 50 per cent profit by only doing three dollars' worth of work." It wasn't long before he got a raise, to $40 a week, but he rarely drew on his salary. There was no need: He was a newspaperman, and whatever he wrote about the mines could, and did, affect their value. Speculators routinely gave Twain presents of shares in their mines, and he found that he could sell these shares and live comfortably off the profits, which he did.

Reporters were given shares on the sensible and generally correct assumption that they would promote the mines in the newspaper — mines in which they themselves now owned stock. And reporters obliged. In the process, Twain learned valuable lessons in what we call branding and marketing. He learned the value of promoting a product, especially when it was worthless, and how to do so persuasively, with cunning. Mine owners didn't care what the papers reported, provided they said *something*.

> Consequently, we generally said a word or two to the effect that the "indications" were good, or that the ledge

was "six feet wide," or that the rock "resembled the Comstock" (and so it did—but as a general thing the resemblance was not startling enough to knock you down). If the rock was moderately promising, we followed the custom of the country, using strong adjectives and frothed at the mouth as if a very marvel in silver discoveries had transpired. If the mine was a "developed" one, and had no pay ore to show (and of course it hadn't), we praised the tunnel, said it was one of the most infatuating tunnels in the land; driveled and driveled about the tunnel till we ran entirely out of ecstasies—but never said a word about the rock.

The reporters "would squander half a column of adulation on a shaft, or a new wire rope, or a dressed pine windlass, or a fascinating force pump, and close with a burst of admiration of the 'gentlemanly and efficient superintendent' of the mine—but never utter a whisper about the rock." Mine owners "were always satisfied. Occasionally, we patched up and varnished our reputation for discrimination and stern, undeviating accuracy, by giving some abandoned claim a blast that ought to have made its dry bones rattle—and then somebody would seize it and sell it on the fleeting notoriety thus conferred upon it."

In such a heady environment, investment money came roaring in, and the price of shares kept pushing skyward. From San Francisco and other cities, even "washerwomen and servant girls" would pool their resources and send agents to buy shares for them. They, too, were only human, no better or worse than the seventeenth-century Dutch chimneysweeps who invested in tulip bulbs or the exotic dancer in the 2015 movie *The Big Short* who bought five houses.

Pretty soon, Twain had amassed boxes of stock certificates,

and, in May 1864, he felt flush enough to resign altogether from the *Territorial Enterprise* and set off for San Francisco himself. For a man accustomed to shanty towns on sagebrush mountainsides, San Francisco "was Paradise to me. I lived at the best hotel, exhibited my clothes in the most conspicuous places, infested the opera, and learned to seem enraptured with music which oftener afflicted my ignorant ear than enchanted it, if I had had the vulgar honesty to confess it."

He had always longed to be a social butterfly, he admitted, and was finally one at last. "I attended private parties in sumptuous evening dress, simpered and aired my graces like a born beau, and polkaed and schottisched with a step peculiar to myself—and the kangaroo." He lived like "a man worth a hundred thousand dollars (prospectively), and likely to reach absolute affluence" as soon as any one of his holdings might make his fortune.

All the while, he held tight. Stocks went on rising. Speculation intensified. Then something unexpected happened—unexpected, that is, to people with what John Kenneth Galbraith called a "vested interest in euphoria"—and refused to see that a so-called growth adjustment was inevitable. The market value of the Comstock mines, which had been $40 million, had fallen to $12 million in the summer of 1863 and then, on December 15, was down to $4 million. The boom went bust. Over the next two years, 10,000 people moved away from Nevada.

"The wreck was complete," Twain recalled. "The bubble scarcely left a microscopic moisture behind it. I was an early beggar and a thorough one. My hoarded stocks were not worth the paper they were printed on. I threw them all away. I, the cheerful idiot that had been squandering money like water, and thought myself beyond the reach of misfortune, had not now fifty dollars when I gathered together my various debts and paid them." He moved out of the hotel and into a modest board-inghouse and took a job as reporter for the *Sacramento Union.*

Orion, meanwhile, had lost his job. When Nevada had en-tered the Union as the thirty-sixth state in 1864, he had been considered a shoo-in to win election as its new secretary of state. Unfortunately, in what Twain called one of Orion's "spasms of virtue," he decided it would be improper to attend the Republican convention where he was to secure the party's nomination, and therefore lost it to someone else. Orion had also taken an anti-whiskey position, which was not popular in the wide-open West. After trying unsuccessfully to support him-self and his family as a lawyer in Carson City, he sold his home at a loss and moved back to Keokuk. There he started a chicken farm.

There was one additional unsettling development in this dif-ficult period. One day Twain picked up the *Territorial Enter-prise* (he kept the clipping but neglected to date it) and read how three San Franciscans had gone to New York City with ore from their mine in Nevada and sold it for $3 million. Twain rec-ognized from the description of the mine that it was the "blind lead" that, for a few precious days, had been his. "Once more, native imbecility had carried the day," he wrote, "and I had lost a million!"

FOR THE NEXT THREE YEARS, he made do with a newspa-perman's pay. He was even gaining some regional notoriety with his satirical stories when he made one final, forlorn at-tempt to strike it rich in the West, this time prospecting for gold in California's Tuolomne County, 100 miles east of San Fran-cisco. From December 1864 through February 1865, he stayed in a cabin on Jackass Hill, one of maybe five such shacks in what had once been a town of 2,000 to 3,000. "When the mines gave out," Twain wrote, "the town fell into decay, and in a few years wholly disappeared—streets, dwellings, shops, everything—and left no sign."

Here the few stragglers who stayed continued to nurse their vain hopes of great wealth as they panned for gold. Twain's duties were humbling. Mostly, he carried water for rinsing out the pans of dirt. At night, the men passed the time swapping yarns. When they were done, Twain would take notes.

Who knows? Someday, he thought, he could write up those stories. People might like to read them.

8

"Poor, Pitiful Business!"

It was at Jackass Hill in early 1865 that Twain heard a story about a gambler and his frog — a shaggy frog story that, once on paper, changed Twain's life. First published by the *Saturday Press,* a New York newspaper, in October 1865, the story was reprinted in various versions in other publications. Within months, it had reached a national audience, leading to Twain's first book, *The Celebrated Jumping Frog of Calaveras County and Other Sketches,* issued in 1867.

Reviews were encouraging. The *New York Herald* called it "a little book full of good hard sense, wit pure, sparkling and sharp as a diamond . . . and humor genial and inexhaustible." Despite encouraging reviews, sales were not good. This, however, was no great disappointment to the author because he never seemed to have expected it to be a commercial success. "I don't believe it will ever pay anything worth a cent," he told his mother at the time of its release. "I published it simply to advertise myself, and not with the hope of making anything out of it."

But in terms of self-promotion — as an exercise in "personal branding," we might say—the frog story was a hit. People found the tale wildly amusing, and editors wanted more from its author. Though still broke and "utterly miserable," Twain told Orion that he had at last stumbled onto a career, though it was one he did not find especially inspiring. Although he had never before felt a real calling for any line of work,

> I *have* had a "call" to literature, of a low order—*i.e.* humorous. It is nothing to be proud of, but it is my strongest suit, & if I were to listen to that maxim of stern *duty* which says that to do right you *must* multiply the one or the two or the three talents which the Almighty entrusts to your keeping, I would long ago have ceased to meddle with things for which I was by nature unfitted & turned my attention to seriously scribbling to excite the laughter of God's creatures. Poor, pitiful business!

Because readers liked his work, the enterprising newspaperman had little difficulty landing plum assignments. In 1866, he sailed to the Sandwich Islands (the Hawaiian Islands, as they are known today), to report on the islands' sugar industry for the *Sacramento Union*. But with his characteristic curiosity and observational genius, he explored the islands and the islanders' culture, wallowing in this exotic respite from his workaday newspapering.

Back in the States, meanwhile, Orion managed—or mismanaged—the family's real estate interests in Tennessee. A year before Twain sailed away (it sometimes took months for news to travel), Herman Camp, a friend of his who had made a small fortune trading in mining stocks and had moved to New York, offered to buy the family land for $200,000. The man wanted to import European immigrants to grow Tennessee grapes on the acreage. Twain had the contracts drawn up and sent them to Orion for his signature. But by the time they arrived, Twain discovered, Orion had taken the pledge.

> The temperance virtue was temporarily upon him in strong force, and he wrote and said he would not be a party to debauching the country with wine. Also, he said how could he know whether Mr. Camp was going to deal fairly and honestly with those poor people from Europe or not? — and so without waiting to find out, he quashed the whole trade, and there it fell, never to be brought to life again. The land, from being suddenly worth two hundred thousand dollars, became as suddenly worth what it was before — nothing, and taxes to pay.

When Twain learned the news, he told Orion's wife, Mollie, he would "never entirely forgive" his brother. If he let the land be sold for taxes, "all his religion will not wipe out the sin. It is no use to quote Scripture to me, Mollie, — I am in poverty and exile now because of Orion's religious scruples. Religion & poverty cannot go together." Orion might save his own soul, "but in doing it he will damn the balance of the family. I want no such religion." It appalled him to think of that land "going to the dogs when I could have sold it & been at home now, instead of drifting about the outskirts of the world, battling for bread." Twain was aware that he might have "made Orion mad, but I don't care a cent."

HAWAII'S OCEAN BREEZES offered some consolation, and Twain's life in poverty was soon to pass. Not content with filing a mere business story, Twain used his time in the South Pacific to write his early travel pieces, first for the *Sacramento Union* and, over the next several months, for other West Coast newspapers. His travel pieces were vivid and candid, and the sketches he wrote merely to amuse were widely read, enjoyed, and talked about. They were so popular that, upon his return to California, he began to give lively lectures about his experiences in Hawaii. More and more editors were becoming aware of his work, and more and more readers recognized his byline and looked forward to his articles.

As Twain's fame rose, he entered an entirely new phase of his life. Over the next few years, he established himself as one of the country's most popular (and well-compensated) lecturers. Bringing his own brand of standup comedy to packed houses coast to coast, he managed, in his own words, to "persecute the public for their lasting benefit & my profit." He wrote the posters advertising his appearances. "Doors open at 7 o'clock," one poster announced. "The trouble to begin at 8." Other speakers tended to be self-serious or bombastic or both; Twain was intimate and self-deprecating. A reviewer for the *Brooklyn Daily Union* described his "quaint, apparently unconcerned manner and comical drawling tone." He could be irreverent, even coarse. Once he offered to demonstrate what he meant by the word "cannibalism," if only someone in the hall would hand him a baby.

The book that established his brand not only throughout the United States but in Europe as well was *The Innocents Abroad*. In 1867, on assignment from the *San Francisco Alta,* Twain sailed to Europe and the Holy Land on the paddle-wheeler *Quaker City,* which carried well-heeled American tourists eager to see the world. That summer and fall, he wrote a series of letters for the *Alta* as well as for the *New York Herald* and *New York Tribune,* describing with disarming candor his response to sights ordinarily treated with reverence. He couldn't stand the

Old Masters, he admitted; shown a Madonna attributed by an
Italian tour guide to St. Luke, Twain "could not help admiring
the Apostle's modesty in never once mentioning in his writings
that he could paint."

The letters caused a sensation, and when Twain returned
from the voyage in November, he was approached by Elisha
Bliss of the American Publishing Company of Hartford, Connecticut. The American Publishing Company was in the subscription book business, which was comparable in its time to
print-on-demand today, and very much like publishing for the
Kindle. Such books were not sold in bookstores—the respectable and dignified way—but by commissioned sales agents
who scoured the countryside, reaching customers who rarely
got to town. These sales agents went farmhouse to farmhouse,
carrying brochures and drumming up advance orders. In the
twenty-five years following the Civil War, three-quarters of all
books purchased in the United States were sold by these
agents.

There was no prestige in subscription publishing, but Bliss
promised Twain wide distribution. "We are perhaps the oldest
subscription house in the country, and have never failed to give
a book an *immense* circulation," Bliss said. Bliss offered Twain
$10,000 for a completed manuscript, or a royalty of 5 percent.
Exercising "the best business judgment I ever displayed," Twain
took the 5 percent.

Released in July 1869, *The Innocents Abroad* was a best-
seller in America and in Europe. The reviews were almost uni-
formly favorable. From William Dean Howells of the tony
Atlantic Monthly, the book received the Eastern literary establishment's version of five stars on Amazon. The book is "very
amusing," Howells wrote. Twain's "is always good-humored
humor," and "even in its impudence it is charming." The *Exam-*

iner and London Review said the book was written in language "full of point and pungency, and abounds in anecdotes of racy humour." *The Innocents Abroad* "makes no pretence to inform or instruct; it is simply meant to amuse, and in that it succeeds to perfection."

The Quaker City excursion did more for Twain than make him famous throughout the English-speaking world and, for a time, prosperous. It also helped him settle on the woman he hoped to marry. Now in his early thirties, he had become eager to find a wife. But he also wanted to make sure he was ready for the responsibilities of a family. In an 1862 letter to Orion's wife, he was forthright about the need to be financially secure.

> I am not married yet, and I never *will* marry until I can afford to have servants enough to leave my wife in the position for which I designed her, viz: as a *companion*. I don't want to sleep with a three-fold Being who is cook, chambermaid and washerwoman all in one. I don't mind sleeping with female servants as long as I am a bachelor —by no means—but *after* I marry, that sort of thing will be "played out," you know.

He discussed the subject with other female confidants as well. "I want a good wife," he told a friend from the *Quaker City* trip. "I want a couple of them if they are particularly good." Maybe his best bet, he went on, was to "swindle some poor girl into marrying me. But I wouldn't expect to be 'worthy' of her. I wouldn't have a girl that *I* was worthy of. *She* wouldn't do. She wouldn't be respectable enough."

9

"It Is Ours—All Ours—Everything"

It was aboard the *Quaker City* that an amiable young man from Elmira, New York, named Charley Langdon showed Twain a miniature portrait of his older sister. Then and there, Twain would claim, he fell in love with the delicate young woman and made up his mind to marry her. "I'll harass that girl and harass her till she'll *have* to say yes!" he told a friend.

Her name was Olivia Langdon. Known to friends and family as Livy, she was not only respectable but rich. Her father was Jervis Langdon, a descendent of a distinguished New England family (one ancestor had been president of Harvard), though self-made in the American tradition. A storekeeper at sixteen, he had invested in timberlands and then coal, eventually owning not only mines but a railroad to transport the coal. Langdon was a pillar of the community, broad-minded in his views and socially progressive. He was an abolitionist whose home, it was said, had been a stop on the Underground Railroad. Like her father, Livy Langdon had a kindly and generous nature, a nascent Lady Bountiful with a social conscience.

Twain arranged to meet Livy and was soon a frequent and eager visitor to the Langdon home, which was like nothing back in Hannibal. The house and grounds occupied an entire city block; as horses and carriages approached, their weight automatically opened three sets of gates. "Huge chandeliers hung from the high ceilings of each room. Sumptuous curtains and plush upholstery gave the home the palatial yet somber, heavy look that the wealthy of the time so desired."

Undaunted by his surroundings—no doubt inspired by them—Twain courted Livy obsessively. This uneducated son of slaveholders, born into obscurity in rural Missouri, a man in his thirties with some fleeting notoriety based on nothing more substantial than a book he had written that some people found amusing, Twain was of course an unlikely suitor. In time, however, Livy, like the rest of America, succumbed to his inimitable charms. In November 1868, she accepted his proposal of marriage.

AS MIGHT BE EXPECTED, Livy's father had misgivings. Hoping to put these reservations to rest, Twain met privately with Langdon, who tactfully explained his position. While Langdon had grown fond of Twain, he barely knew his prospective son-in-law, who was a stranger not only in the town but in the entirety of the East. As part of his due diligence, Langdon asked Twain for the names of men who might vouch for Twain's "character, in case I had one." Twain furnished those of six "prominent" men. Langdon wrote to them all, and when their replies arrived, he met with Twain again.

In their meeting, Langdon read the letters aloud. All those men "were frank to a fault," Twain said. "They not only spoke in disapproval of me but they were quite unnecessarily and exaggeratedly enthusiastic about it." One said Twain "would fill a drunkard's grave." Another said he was "born to be hung."

Langdon put down the letters, and the silence that followed, Twain said, "consisted largely of sadness and solemnity. I couldn't think of anything to say."

Finally Langdon raised his head. He looked Twain in the eye and asked, "What kind of people are those? Haven't you a friend in the world?"

"Apparently not."

Again there was silence.

"I'll be your friend myself," Langdon said. "Take the girl. I know you better than they do."

In the months leading up to the marriage, hoping to make sure his daughter would be financially sound, Langdon lent Twain $25,000 to buy a third share in a newspaper, the *Buffalo Daily Express*. More than a mere reporter and freelance writer, and more than an editor, Langdon's son-in-law would be an owner of the newspaper, with a stake in the community, instant respectability, and the beginnings of a stock portfolio.

Langdon even discussed buying the Tennessee land from Twain's family. Langdon offered them $20,000 in cash and another $10,000 in stocks for the property and the coal underneath it. That's six times what Orion believed the land was worth, and he had ethical reservations about any such sale. He was reluctant to sell to Langdon at any price. Without explanation, he let it be known that he feared Twain would "unconsciously cheat" his future father-in-law, and the deal fell through.

Mark and Livy were married on February 2, 1870, at the Langdon mansion. When the reception was over, the bride and

groom and rest of the wedding party took off by train for Buffalo. There the newlyweds were to make their home. Upon their
arrival, they were taken by horse-drawn sleigh to a boarding-
house a friend of Twain's had found for them. The other members of the party followed, also in sleighs. Losing contact with
the rest of the group, the sleigh carrying the bride and groom
rolled on and on until Twain, fearing they were lost, grew exas-
perated. Finally, the coachman pulled to a stop in front of a
house on the city's most fashionable street. "People who can
afford to live in this sort of style won't take boarders," Twain
muttered.

Unfazed, Livy led her husband into the brightly lit house,
where, to Twain's befuddlement, the wedding guests were waiting. Again he grumbled that his friend had "put us into a boarding-house whose terms [were] far out of my reach."

Livy put her hand on her husband's arm.

"Don't you understand?" she asked. "It is ours—all ours—
everything—a gift from father!"

The mansion was fully furnished. In on the secret, Livy had
done the decorating. It was also fully staffed, with servants, including a cook and a uniformed coachman. Then there was another gift, in a small box Langdon carried. He opened it and
handed them the deed. Twain was on the verge of tears. Mo-
mentarily (and uncharacteristically) speechless, he rallied sufficiently to put his gratitude into words.

"Mr. Langdon," Twain said. "Whenever you are in Buffalo,
if it's twice a year, come right here. Bring your bag and stay
overnight if you want to. It shan't cost you a cent."

10

"In Fairyland"

The first months of Twain's marriage were among the most enriching of his life. He adored his wife, his fame was increasing, and for the first time ever he had money to burn. By all accounts, his marriage was a happy one, which produced four children—a son, Langdon, who died before his second birthday, and three daughters—Susy, born in 1870; Clara in 1874; and Jean in 1880. Reverting to the name by which close friends and family still knew him, Twain described himself shortly after the wedding as "Little Sammy in Fairyland."

People are "most credulous when they are most happy," Walter Bagehot, the editor of *The Economist,* observed in 1873, and Twain was exactly like all of us when things are going well. Believing almost anything was possible, he came up with what he described as "the pet scheme of my life." Encouraged by the success of *The Innocents Abroad,* he decided to write a first-person account of the South African diamond strike of 1868, but with a catch. Someone else would do the actual experiencing for him. Twain would just write it all up. He told Elisha Bliss of the American Publishing Company about the idea. Bliss was interested. The other person Twain wanted to bring into the project was a friend from his San Francisco days, a clever newspaperman named John Riley. Riley was interested, too.

The plan was for Riley to go to South Africa, with Twain footing all expenses. For three months, Riley would "skirmish, prospect, work, travel & take pretty minute notes." He could even keep any diamonds he found, with this condition: If the diamonds were worth more than $5,000, Twain would get half. Once back in America, Riley was to live at Twain's house, given room and board plus $50 a month, with Twain "to furnish the cigars." There the two would talk about Riley's South African adventures and, within a matter of weeks, Twain would bang out a 600-page book, which Bliss would publish. The first run of 50,000 copies, Twain told Riley, will "sweep the world like a besom of destruction (if you know what that is)." Riley would get "a chance to pick up a fortune in 3 months—the very same chance that thousands would be glad to take at their *own* expense."

Riley would get no share of the book sales. But that was okay, Twain assured him, because "I can slam you into the lecture field for life & secure you ten thousand dollars a year for as long as you live." He would even let Riley in on the *"dead sure tricks"* of the lecturing racket. With Twain's coaching, Riley could easily make $1,200 to $1,500 in a single night, at least in a big market like San Francisco. Riley could pull down $50,000 a year on the lecture circuit. He could pocket an equal amount of profit from the diamonds themselves. The plan is "sound as a drum—there isn't a leak in it," Twain said. "But hurry now. There is no single moment of time to lose . . . I'll have you so well known in 18 months that there will be no man so ignorant as to have to ask, 'Who is Riley?'"

To Bliss, Twain explained that he would write the book "just as if I had been through it all myself, but will explain in the preface that this is done merely to give it life." All he needed from Bliss was a contract and an advance of a thousand dollars. The book will "have a perfectly beautiful sale," he assured the publisher. Even in the extremely unlikely event that Riley never made it back from South Africa—drowned at sea or eaten by lions or something—and the book did not materialize, Twain would just whip out a different 600-page book *"in place of it."* In that case, Bliss could simply deduct the $1,000 advance on the diamond book from that of the substitute. "Don't you see?" Twain said. "You get a *book,* in any event." But speed was essential: "Say yes or no quick, Bliss, for this thing is brim-full of fame & fortune for both author [&] publisher. Expedition's the word, & I don't want any timidity or hesitancy now." Riley "will be packing his trunk by this time tomorrow." Bliss said yes.

In January 1871, Riley set off for South Africa's diamond fields. But things did not work out quite as planned. About 250 miles from Capetown, Riley's steamer ran aground, taking on four feet of water. Riley managed to make it to shore, but the ordeal was one he swore he would not repeat "for one hundred thousand dollars." He then spent the required three months in South Africa but found no diamonds.

And by the time of Riley's return, his South African expedition was no longer high on Twain's to-do list. He was now absorbed in another book, the one that became *Roughing It.* "Let the diamond fever swell and sweat," he told his erstwhile protégé. "We'll try to catch it at the right moment." They could get to work on Riley's book in the summer of 1872, he said. With a stenographer at their side, "we'll all light our cigars every morning, and with your notes before you, we'll talk and yarn, and laugh and weep over your adventures, and the said reporter will take it *all* down." Within a week or two, Twain figured he would have Riley "pumped dry."

Summer came and went, and Riley's health began to fail. On his way back to the United States, he had managed to stab himself with a fork and contracted blood poisoning. Once home, he was diagnosed with cancer and was soon in no condition to work. In June, Twain signed another deal with Bliss—for a travel book about England. In August, Twain sailed for England. In September, Riley died—and the England book was never written.

And as Twain and Bliss had agreed, the publisher applied the advance on the diamond book to the next one.

WHAT'S SIGNIFICANT ABOUT the diamond book fiasco, writes Twain biographer Justin Kaplan, is that Twain envisioned an entire series of works in which another person lived through various adventures while he, as a kind of uber–ghost writer, would put the excitement down on paper. Twain was already famous, so his name on the cover would guarantee sales.

He was like "a rural tinker with a box of gears, pulleys, and pendulums under his bed who thinks he has discovered perpetual motion," Kaplan observed. Twain saw himself on the verge of "rationalizing literary production, of industrializing it, in fact, in order to turn out like so many gold bars stamped 'Mark Twain,' an endless stream of sequels to *The Innocents Abroad*." Whatever flaws it might have had (in "recognition of the unpredictable," for example), the scheme did not lack for "a kind of technological grandeur."

Technological grandeur was never far from Twain's thinking—or his family's. After all, he was born into a family of tinkerers. The patriarch, John Marshall Clemens, had his perpetual-motion machine, while Orion Clemens worked for much of his life on a flying machine. In 1870, Orion was at work on at least five inventions, or what he thought were inventions. There was a wood-sawing machine, a knife of some sort, a wheel-and-chain gizmo for powering paddle-wheel boats, a brake for railroads that Twain estimated could earn his brother $250,000 a year, and (this author's favorite) an "anti-sun-stroke hat." None of these was ever patented, at least not by Orion. (Only a year earlier, a twenty-two-year-old named George Westinghouse *did* receive a patent for a comparable brake that became the industry standard, leading to Westinghouse's immense fortune.)

Twain, who regarded inventors with something like awe, encouraged Orion to keep tinkering. "An inventor is a poet—a true poet—and nothing in any degree less than a high order of poet," he told Pamela. And, as an artist, only the inventor can understand

> or appreciate the *legitimate* "success" of his achievement, littler minds being able to get no higher than a comprehension of a vulgar moneyed success—We would all rejoice to see Orion achieve a moneyed success with his inventions, of course—but if he can, eventually, do something great, something imperial, it were better to do that & starve than not to do it at all.

Even a device Twain referred to as Orion's "modest little drilling machine" held great promise. It "shows the presence of the patrician blood of intellect . . . which separates its possessor from the common multitude & marks him as one not beholden to the caprices of politics but endowed with greatness in his own right."

Such uncharacteristically puffed-up prose leads the reader to wonder what Twain took the next morning for his hangover.

WHILE ORION FIDDLED with his inventions, Twain was at work on one of his own—one that, while less grandiose than Orion's flying machine, had practical applications and actually did get patented. Twain got the idea in mid-December 1870 when he was paying a call on John Hay, then an editorial writer for the *New York Tribune*. Twain had entered the *Tribune* office and accidently barged in on Hay's boss, who was hard at work on some literary composition of his own. Hay's boss was Horace Greeley. As the paper's founder and editor, Greeley "had the reputation of being pretty plain with strangers who interrupted his train of thought."

Greeley did not disappoint. "Well, what in hell do *you* want!" he barked.

"I was looking for a gentlem—"

"Don't keep them in stock—clear out!"

Twain said he "could have made a very neat retort, but didn't, for I was flurried and didn't think of it till I was down stairs."

Twain's first impression of Greeley was that his reputation for impatience was well earned. But his second impression, which Twain passed along to the U.S. Patent Office, was that Greeley was wearing "the most extraordinary set of trowsers [*sic*]." Greeley's trousers stuck half in and half out of his boots in a disorderly and uncomfortable way that Twain could never quite unsee. So he immediately went to work trying to figure out "some plan for making them hang more gracefully."

The answer came to Twain in one of those famous "a-ha!" moments that brain scientists these days study and innovation-mad business leaders profess to want more of. But of course, as

we now know, these moments usually occur only after an indi-
vidual has devoted years of research and investigation to a spe-
cific problem. All high achievers devote at least 10,000 hours to
whatever it is they are trying to accomplish, according to Malcolm Gladwell. But that wasn't the case with Twain. Meaning
no disrespect, Twain was not a professional fashion designer,
and by all evidence, he had invested maybe one or two hours,
tops.

To appreciate the full magnitude of Twain's contribution to
a field in which he had no training whatsoever, it is important
to know something more about life as it was experienced during
this time by the pants-wearing men of the world. Belts, though
in existence since the Bronze Age, were largely decorative. And
pants worn by men in Twain's day were so high-waisted that
belts were nearly useless. Suspenders as we know them were not
in use until 1820, and Twain, like many men, found them uncomfortable. (It was only in World War I that men became comfortable with uniform belts and then with belts in civilian life.)

And so, with all this buzzing about in Twain's mind, he
would apparently lie awake at night, worrying about Horace
Greeley's pants. Then one morning, unable to get back to sleep,
Twain suddenly thought of an elastic strap. It just snapped into
his mind, as elastic tends to do. Like Archimedes leaping naked
from his bath, Twain jumped out of bed.

"While I dressed, it occurred to me that in order to be efficient, the strap must be *adjustable* & *detachable,* when the
wearer did not wish it to be *permanent,*" he recalled. "So I de-
vised the plan of having two or three button-holes in each end
of the strap, & *buttoning* it to the garment—whereby it could
be shortened or removed at pleasure." He began to sketch diagrams of his idea. As he told the Patent Office: "While washing
(these details seem a little trivial, I grant, but they are *history* &

therefore in some degree respect-worthy,)" he drew other diagrams. He then showed the sketches to Orion and, in the course of their conversation, "it occurred to me that this invention would apply to ladies' stays." This led to yet another diagram. Then—*mirabile dictu!*—Twain realized the device might be used on shirts and underwear, too. The possibilities were endless.

Swelled up with confidence, Twain went to Washington in October 1871 and, in December, secured U.S. Patent 121,992. There was a dispute from another applicant, but Twain prevailed after agreeing to allow the other man a share in the profits once the device was manufactured and marketed. But as it turned out, Twain never manufactured it, and in 1877, the other man sued Twain, seeking $10,000 for breach of contract. Finding for the plaintiff, the court awarded him only $300. More than a century later, Twain's elastic strap was praised in an unlikely source. In 2011, Rebecca Greenfield wrote in the venerable *Atlantic:*

> While the literature claims [Twain's invention] is most useful for "vests, pantaloons or other garments requiring straps," how many pantaloons do you see with elastic straps held together by clasps these days? This clever invention only caught on with one snug garment: the bra. For those with little brassiere experience, not a button, not a strap, but a clasp is all that secures that elastic band, which holds up women's breasts. So not-so-dexterous ladies and gents, you can thank Mark Twain for that.

Greenfield, moreover, imagined additional uses for the device. "We should refocus and bring this invention back to where

Twain intended it to be: 'vests, pantaloons or other garments requiring straps.' Just think: Stretchy pants with clasps."

OF COURSE THE FIRST MONTHS of Twain's married life were not all adjustable elastic straps. There were adjustments of other kinds, too. Twain soon grew bored with newspaper office routine. Fred Kaplan in his Twain biography puts it nicely: "Taking full advantage of his ownership prerogatives, he began to stay away from the *Express* office."

Livy, meanwhile, never really felt at home in Buffalo and missed her family. Her homesickness intensified in the spring, when her father fell seriously ill. On August 6, 1870, just eight months after his daughter's wedding, Jervis Langdon died. While sad and unsettling—Twain had come to love his father-in-law—Langdon's death also opened up new opportunities for the newlyweds. Langdon left his fortune to be divided among his widow and their two children, Livy and her brother, Charley. An adopted daughter, Susan Crane, was given a country house called Quarry Farm, overlooking Elmira. Twain and his bride inherited $250,000—in our time, about $4,400,000.

11

"To Live in This Style . . ."

By the spring of 1871, little more than a year after arriving in Buffalo, Twain and Livy decided to leave. They sold the house they had been given as a wedding present, at a loss. They also sold their share in the newspaper, also at a loss. Then they moved to Hartford, Connecticut.

Twain had first visited Hartford in 1868. These days, we think of the city as a center of the American insurance business, which it has been ever since J. P. Morgan's grandfather established the Aetna Fire Insurance Company there in 1817. But Hartford was headquarters as well of Sharps Rifle Manufacturing Company and the Colt Armory, which manufactured firearms. It was also home to the Pratt & Whitney Company, which produced machine tools. The city was prosperous, and Twain was understandably impressed. "Hartford dollars have a place in half the great moneyed enterprises of the union," he reported in the *Alta California*.

Twain also found Hartford attractive because it was a hub

of the subscription book business. His own publisher, Elisha Bliss of the American Publishing Company, was still headquartered in the city, which also counted among its residents a number of financially comfortable and socially progressive intellectuals. Henry Ward Beecher, Charles Dudley Warner, Harriet Beecher Stowe, and other advanced thinkers made their homes in Nook Farm, a close-knit woodsy enclave that appealed to Twain's social as well as financial ambitions. The houses were "not shingle-shaped affairs, stood on end and packed together like a 'deck' of cards, but massive private hotels," with spacious yards. "To live in this style," Twain said, "one must have his bank account, of course."

A skeptic in religious matters, Twain even felt comfortable among the city's educated, broad-minded, and very worldly churchgoers. He called the community's Congregational house of worship "the Church of the Holy Speculators." Its pastor, Joseph Twichell, became one of his closest friends. Twichell was "one of the best of men," Twain said, "although a clergyman." Kenneth Andrews in *Nook Farm: Mark Twain's Hartford Circle* says Twichell could have "castigated [his congregants for] their devotion to prosperity, and led them from the dominant commercialism" of their age. But this never occurred to Twichell, because he was a man of his time and place, "entirely normal and nothing neurotic."

The same could not be said of their neighbor Harriet Beecher Stowe. A crusader on behalf of noble causes, the author of *Uncle Tom's Cabin* became increasingly eccentric with age. When Twain knew her, she would wander into somebody else's house, slip up behind an unsuspecting neighbor who might be lost in thought or reading a book, and "fetch a whoop that would jump that person out of his skin."

• • •

TWAIN AND LIVY decided to build a house in Hartford and "build it right even if it does cost 25 percent more." Twenty-five percent more than what, Twain didn't say, but whatever sum he had in mind, the house ended up costing a great deal more than that. Construction seemed to take forever, and the family moved in before the house was finished. "The carpenters are here for time & eternity," Twain said. "I kill them when I get opportunities, but the builder goes & gets more." He was determined to get all the workers off the property as soon as possible, "even if we have to import an epidemic to do it."

Twain was nonetheless delighted with the results of their work, which he called "the loveliest home that ever was." Even today, the twenty-five-room, thirteen-fireplace, seven-bath mansion is a showstopper, though it has never been without its detractors. The *Hartford Times* said it was "one of the oddest-looking buildings . . . ever designed for dwelling." The *Elmira Advertiser* called it a "brick-kiln gone crazy, the outside ginger-breaded with woodwork, as a baker sugar-ornaments the top and side of a fruit loaf."

With furnishings from all over the world, the interior was no less eye-popping. A carved chimney piece was from a castle in Scotland. Pierced brass plates around the fireplace in the marble-floored entrance hall were from India. There was a window over one of the fireplaces so the family could enjoy a cozy fire while watching snow fall. Louis Comfort Tiffany, son of the New York jeweler, had a hand in the front-hall decoration. In Venice, Livy found the master bedroom's walnut bed frame with carved cherubs. "This Italy does tempt money out of one's pocket," Livy told her mother. After another European shopping spree, the family returned with twenty-two freight boxes of furnishings for the house. They accumulated so much stuff that much of it had to go immediately into storage.

Over the years, Twain gave a number of estimates of the cost of the house, a new barn, and a carriage house. The lowest was $110,000, and the highest was $167,000 in the dollars of the day. In 1877, soon after the family moved in, the city assigned the property's value at $66,650, equivalent to $1,420,000 today. Three years later, they began renovations, enlarging the kitchen and front hall. Once that was done, Twain said, they "still had a little cash left over, on account of the plumber not knowing it." But give the plumber his due: The house had running water, a shower, and indoor toilets. When William Dean Howells brought his son to visit, the boy was duly impressed. Finding red soap in one of the bathrooms, he cried out, "Why, they've even got their soap painted!"

In 1902, long after Twain and his family had moved away and the house stood uninhabited for several years, it was purchased by a Hartford insurance executive for $28,800. In 1920, he sold the house to a real estate investor (with two undertakers as partners) for $55,000. When these investors announced plans to demolish the house and replace it with apartments, civic-minded Hartford residents were incensed. The developer's response was to offer it to any literary types for $300,000. If they didn't buy the property at that price, he would "take off that ugly roof" and stack three more stories on the house. In 1925, the developer sold it for $82,000, and the house was acquired in 1929 for use as a museum, visitor center, and library for $150,000. The Mark Twain House & Museum opened in 2003.

A FLESH-AND-BLOOD SOCIAL NETWORKING MACHINE, Twain made the most of the intellectual and commercial opportunities that Hartford presented. He and Livy opened their house to authors, publishers, bankers, merchants, politicians, and other civic leaders, sparing no expense in making their events memorable. Daughter Clara Clemens remembered her parents "constantly preparing for lunch parties and dinner parties." Howells recalled them as "whole-souled hosts, with inextinguishable money, and a palace of a house."

They spent as much as $100 a week on food and drink and their accoutrements, or about $100,000 a year at today's values. A maid remembered the dinner parties as elaborate affairs, where all sorts of delicacies were served. There was ice cream, for example, and "never plain ordinary ice cream—we always had our ice cream put up in some wonderful shapes—like flowers or cherubs, little angels—all different kinds and different shapes and colors—oh, everything lovely!"

HAPPY IN HARTFORD, Twain was energetic and productive. He worked on some of the books that made him a literary lion in the third-floor combination billiard room and study, where, during most of the year, he did his writing. In the summer, he turned out hundreds of pages from an outdoor study built especially for him at Quarry Farm by Livy's sister by adoption, Susan Crane, and her husband. "It is octagonal, with a peaked roof, each octagon filled with a spacious window," Twain wrote, "and it sits perched in complete isolation on top of an elevation that commands leagues of valley and city and retreating ranges of distant blue hills."

It was during the Hartford years that Twain wrote *Roughing It* and *The Adventures of Tom Sawyer*. It was also during this period that Twain and his neighbor Charles Dudley Warner collaborated on *The Gilded Age*. Published in 1873, *The Gilded Age* was never one of Twain's most popular novels, but it has the distinction of giving the era of the great robber barons its name. Sales of these three Twain books were not as brisk as those of *The Innocents Abroad*, though they still sold well. *Tom*

Sawyer would have been more of a commercial success had not "Canadian pirates," as Twain called them, flooded the U.S. market with bootleg copies. He made nothing from the sales of these unauthorized editions and was appropriately aggrieved, leading to a longtime interest in and advocacy of copyright protection for authors.

But *The Gilded Age* made money for the author in a way no one anticipated. In the early 1870s, Twain learned of an unauthorized version of *The Gilded Age* being performed on the stage. Understandably indignant that someone else was profiting from his work, Twain considered suing the scoundrel who wrote and produced the bootleg production but instead simply bought the rights to the play outright, declaring "he shan't run any play on MY brains." Twain revised the play and renamed it *Colonel Sellers,* after the big-talking promoter who dominates the story. The play toured for a decade, earning more money for Twain than the novel ever did.

The book that was most profitable during the Hartford years was one Twain didn't write but *invented*. The book, according to Albert Bigelow Paine, "did not contain a single word that critics could praise or condemn." This was Mark Twain's Self-Pasting Scrap Book. The idea first occurred to him in the summer of 1872 and represented a response to a market demand, even if consumers were not yet aware that any such demand existed.

An avid collector of newspaper clippings about himself, Twain evidently seethed with annoyance whenever the clippings were torn or smudged or otherwise defaced—especially when he tried to affix them to scrapbook pages. On the reasonable assumption that others had been subjected to similar frustrations, he envisioned a scrapbook whose pages were coated with what Ron Powers calls a "gum-stickum, to ward off the heartache of brittle, ink-sucking mucilage." As Twain explained to his brother Orion, "you need not wet any more of the gum than your scrap or scraps will cover," and—*voilà!*—"you may shut up the book and the leaves won't stick together."

Eager to make sure his patent application was not challenged by another inventor, Twain instructed Orion to preserve the envelope from the letter in which he laid out the plan, because the postmark "ought to be good evidence of the date of this great humanizing and civilizing invention." There was no challenge, and in June 1873, the scrapbook was awarded U.S. Patent 140,245.

Orion showed little interest in the scrapbook. This was unusual, Powers writes, because Orion was ordinarily as "malleable as a spaniel." But a friend from the *Quaker City* excursion was very much interested. This was Dan Slote of Slote, Woodman and Company, a New York City stationery-supply company. Among the pious pilgrims on the *Quaker City,* Twain and Slote forged an instantaneous bond. Slote, who packed 3,000 cigars for the voyage, became Twain's "splendid, immoral, tobacco-smoking, wine-drinking, godless room-mate" on the trip. Together, they formed the core of "the unholiest gang that ever cavorted through Palestine," horrifying their sanctimonious shipmates with their irreverence. Back in the United States, Twain would stay at Slote's house during visits to Manhattan, where they dedicated every Saturday "as a solemn fast-day," Twain told his mother and sister. On such occasions, "we will entertain no light matters or frivolous conversations, but only get drunk."

WHEN TWAIN BROUGHT Slote the idea for the scrapbook, Slote's company agreed to produce and distribute the finished product. The scrapbook sold 25,000 copies that first year, earning Twain $12,000, or $231,000 in our day. In time, there were more than fifty varieties to choose from. Some estimates have Twain pocketing $50,000 from the scrapbook, or about $1,100,000 today. But for some unknown reason, still he persuaded himself that Slote was swindling him. This suspicion was strengthened in July 1878, when Slote asked Twain to lend the company $5,000 at 7 percent interest. Twain recalled the negotiation this way:

> As security he offered the firm's note. I asked for an endorser. He was much surprised and said that if endorsers were handy and easy to get at he wouldn't have come to me for the money, he could get it anywhere. That seemed reasonable, and so I gave him the five thousand dollars.

Three days after Twain made the loan, Slote, Woodman and Company went out of business.

12

"How the Ignorant
and Inexperienced Succeed"

Twain, being Twain, did not confine his business activities to the scrapbook alone. As a prominent citizen of Hartford, he of course invested in an insurance company. Here's how *Harper's Weekly*, in its July 4, 1874, issue, reported this latest venture:

> Mr. Samuel L. Clemens, sometime [*sic*] known as "Mark Twain," has at last found his true mission. From idling away his time as a writer he has determined to become an underwriter—one of those practical money-absorbing men for whom Hartford is a sort of hive, so to speak. The cash citizens of Hartford have resolved to get a new accident insurance company, of which it is surmised that Mr. Clemens who will be a stockholder is to be made "Old Prex." He has met with a great many accidents in his [day] and now proposes to go into it as a matter of statistics and income.

Twain was never made president of the new Hartford Accident Insurance Company, although he did serve on its board of
directors. Established to compete with Traveler's, the new company was the brainchild of John Percival Jones, a "big-hearted
man with ninety-nine parts of him pure generosity," as Twain
described him. Jones had struck it rich in the Comstock Lode
and now represented Nevada in the U.S. Senate. A man of far-
flung business interests, Jones was a founder of Santa Monica,
California, and built the first railroad linking that city with Los
Angeles.

Assured by Jones's business associates that Twain could not
possibly lose any money on the investment, Twain purchased
$50,000 of stock in the Hartford Accident Insurance Company
and attended every board meeting for a year and a half. He was
also an eager spokesman for the company—what today we
might call a passionate "brand ambassador." At a dinner for
other Hartford businessmen in October 1874, for example,
Twain spoke on behalf of the entire industry:

> Certainly there is no nobler field for human effort than
> the insurance line of business—especially accident insur-
> ance. Ever since I have been a director in an accident-in-
> surance company I have felt that I am a better man. Life
> has seemed more precious. Accidents have assumed a
> kindlier aspect. Distressing special providences have lost
> half their horror. I look upon a cripple now with affec-
> tionate interest—as an advertisement.

Poetry had lost its allure, Twain discovered; he no longer
found politics interesting. "But to me now," he said, "there is a
charm about a railroad collision that is unspeakable."

As for the Hartford Accident Insurance Company, Twain described it as "an institution which is peculiarly to be depended upon. A man is bound to prosper who gives it his custom. No man can take out a policy in it and not get crippled before the year is out."

UNFORTUNATELY, the Hartford Accident Insurance Company proved less dependable than Twain had hoped. At the end of eighteen months, the company "went to pieces and I was out of pocket twenty-three thousand dollars." That's about $495,000 today. But when it came time to collect what the company owed him, Twain was told (again by associates) that Jones was temporarily "straitened and would be glad if I would wait a while" for repayment. This seemed reasonable, Twain decided, because he knew Jones had recently established

> a line of artificial ice-house factories clear across the Southern States—nothing like it this side of the great Wall of China. I knew that the factories had cost him a million dollars or so, and that the people down there hadn't been trained to admire ice and didn't want any or wouldn't buy any—that therefore the Chinese Wall was an entire loss and failure.

Twain was also aware that another of the senator's investments—the St. James Hotel at Broadway and Twenty-sixth Street in Manhattan—was going bust, because of the big-hearted man's inexhaustible generosity. There were no vacancies for this simple reason: Instead of renting rooms to paying guests, Jones had filled the hotel "from roof to cellar with poor relations gathered from the four corners of the earth—plumbers, bricklayers, unsuccessful clergymen, and in fact, all the different kinds of people that knew nothing about the hotel business." All these non-paying guests, apparently, camped out at the hotel, "waiting for Jones to find lucrative occupations for them."

Twain was also painfully aware that the assurance that he would be repaid for his investment in the company had not come from Jones himself but through Jones's surrogates. It took six months for Jones to learn that Twain had been seeking repayment, and Jones was appalled that Twain had not been paid. Jones wrote a check for $23,000 on the spot. "There are not many John P. Joneses in the world," Twain said.

MADE WHOLE BY JONES, Twain "was prepared to seek sudden fortune again," he recalled. "The reader, deceived by what I have been saying about my adventures, will jump to the conclusion that I sought an opportunity at once. I did nothing of the kind. I was the burnt child. I wanted nothing further to do with speculations."

And it's true. Twain showed remarkable, uncharacteristic, maybe even superhuman restraint. In the spring of 1877, with the check for $23,000 burning a hole in his pocket, Twain was summoned to the office of the *Hartford Courant* to witness a demonstration of an invention installed for the newspaper's use. The inventor had sent an agent to represent the company that was marketing the invention and to sell shares in it. "He believed there was great fortune in store for it and wanted me to take some stock. I declined. I said I didn't want anything more to do with wildcat speculation." The agent kept reducing the price; Twain kept refusing to buy. "He became eager — insisted I take five hundred dollars' worth. He said he would sell me as much as I wanted for five hundred dollars — offered to let me gather it up in my hands and measure it in a plug hat — said

I could have a whole hatful for five hundred dollars." Still he resisted.

That invention was the telephone. The agent was an associate of Alexander Graham Bell's. He represented the National Bell Telephone Company, which had been formed the previous March, capitalized at $850,000. Its share price in June, shortly after Twain chose not to invest, was $110. By December, the value had shot up to $995. (In fairness to Twain, even Western Union did not see the telephone's potential, declining an offer to buy the patent from Bell. "The device," the company said, "is inherently of no value to us.")

So the telephone salesman struck out with Twain but succeeded with an old Hartford dry-goods clerk who sank his entire life savings of $5,000 into Bell Telephone stock. The next time Twain saw the old man, about a year later, he "was driving around in a sumptuous barouche with liveried servants all over it in piles—and his telephone stock was emptying greenbacks into his premises at such a rate that he had to handle them with a shovel. It is strange the way the ignorant and inexperienced so often and so undeservedly succeed when the informed and deserving fail."

SOME OF THE MAN'S EARNINGS surely came from Twain because he became a Bell Telephone customer himself. Later that year, Twain had a telephone installed in his own home, "the *first one* that was ever used in a private house in the world." This is a difficult claim to prove, but so far no one seems to have refuted it. Twain was the kind of man who doesn't believe a product has much value, but then finds it necessary to buy one for himself.

Twain was always of two minds about this new technology. For business purposes, a telephone could be useful. The line he installed to the telegraph office in Hartford was "like adding a hundred servants to one's staff for a cent apiece for a week." It was good for summoning a doctor if a member of the household needed care. But the telephone was also a "profanity-breeding" source of endless annoyance and interruption. Most of what people wanted to use it for was talking nonsense. Its ringing must have also been an unpleasant reminder of the fortune he had forgone by refusing to invest in it. Twain seems to have borne Alexander Graham Bell no ill will personally, but he often wondered if the telephone was not, on balance, a curse.

In a holiday greeting issued a few winters later, Twain wrote: "It is my heart-warm and world-embracing Christmas hope and aspiration that all of us, the high, the low, the rich, the poor, the admired, the despised, the loved, the hated, the civilized, the savage (every man and brother of us all through-out the whole earth), may eventually be gathered together in a heaven of everlasting peace and bliss, except the inventor of the telephone."

13

"A Lie & a Fraud"

Twain's next business partner of note—after Dan Slote, the scrapbook impresario—was Frank Fuller, another friend from his days out West. Twain and Fuller had met in Virginia City in 1862. Fuller, who worked as a dentist, newspaperman, insurance salesman, speculator in mining stocks, and health food wholesaler, had been Twain's booking agent for his first lectures in San Francisco.

Fuller had also been a supplier of what Twain liked to call "cundrums," which was his facetious misspelling for his favorite contraceptive device. In 1868, Fuller was "making money hand over fist in the manufacture of a patented, odorless India rubber cloth, which is coming greatly into fashion for buggy tops and such things." It was the other things that interested Twain. He asked Fuller to send him "one dozen Odorless Rubber Cundrums—I don't mind them being odorless—I can supply the odor myself. I would like to have your picture on them." That was in August. Twain still hadn't received the shipment in

September but told Fuller not to fret. "I can get along without them, I suppose. My aunt never uses them."

Fuller's latest venture was what Twain called "an engine or a furnace or something of the kind which would get out 99 per cent of all the steam that was in a pound of coal." They called it the Vaporizer, and Twain invested $5,000 in the New York Vaporizer Company. Experts scoffed at the idea that the Vaporizer could do what Fuller and Twain said it could, but the two partners were unfazed. Determined to prove the technology, Twain took the idea to Charles B. Richards, a mechanical engineer at the Colt Armory in Hartford, for his assessment:

> He was a specialist and knew all about coal and steam. He seemed to be doubtful about this machine and I asked him why. He said, because the amount of steam concealed in a pound of coal was known to be a fraction and that my inventor was mistaken about his 99 per cent. He showed me a printed book of solid pages of figures, figures that made me drunk and dizzy. He showed me that my man's machine couldn't come within 90 per cent of doing what it proposed to do. I went away a little discouraged.

Discouraged, but not defeated. Twain responded to Richards's opinion by hiring the inventor, one H. C. Bowers, to build a prototype, "on a salary of thirty-five dollars a week, I to pay all expenses." Under their arrangement, there was no incentive to get the job done promptly, Parkinson's Law stating, of course, that work expands so as to fill the time available for its completion. This is especially the case when there is no deadline.

What with frequent visits, when the inventor reported on his progress, it took Bowers "a good many weeks" to build the Vaporizer. Early on Twain noticed by his contractor's "breath and gait that he was spending thirty-six dollars a week on whisky, and I couldn't ever find out where he got the other dollar." Finally, "the machine was finished, but it wouldn't go. It did save 1 percent of the steam that was in a pound of coal, but that was nothing. You could do it with a tea-kettle."

Twain had seen enough of the Vaporizer. "So I threw the thing away and looked around for something fresh." By now, however, Twain had become an "enthusiast on steam" and invested in a Hartford company that "proposed to make and sell and revolutionize everything with a new kind of steam pulley." Twain never said much more about this venture. Maybe that's because he didn't like to think about it. He did say this, though: "The steam pulley pulled thirty-two thousand dollars out of my pocket in sixteen months, then went to pieces and I was alone in the world again, without an occupation."

ALONE IN THE WORLD without work is an exaggeration, of course, but it is not difficult to see why Twain felt the way he did. He and Livy had two daughters now, and they were running seriously low on funds. The Panic of 1873 took a significant bite out of the coal business and, therefore, out of Livy's earnings. Strikes in the coal mines further reduced her income. Twain's investments were also eating into their once-considerable wealth, and after only two years in their new house, they came to realize that they could no longer live in the style to which they had become accustomed in Hartford.

They decided that taking up residence in Europe would be cheaper, or at least less embarrassing, than remaining in Hartford and trying to keep up appearances. So in April 1878, they closed up the mansion and sailed for Germany on the *Holsatia*. For the next eighteen months, they were renters — in Germany,

Switzerland, Italy, France, Belgium, Holland, and England. Twain worked on another travel book, *A Tramp Abroad*, while Livy went shopping, amassing more furnishings for their house back in Hartford. In June 1878, when the coal business seemed to show signs of a temporary recovery, Twain told William Dean Howells, "We've quit being poor." Of course, "poor" must be read here in relative terms: Twain and Livy ate in the best restaurants, socialized nonstop, and hired private tutors for their girls.

Occasionally, Livy would receive spending money from her mother back in Elmira. It was fun to shop, Livy told her, "if other people are to pay for the things that I get—then there's no drawback to the buying." Still, she fretted about having "such an expensive establishment" and worried about "the prospect of not having money." She and Twain didn't always agree about how to spend the money they still had. In April 1879, about six months before their return to America with all their new possessions in tow, Livy wanted to buy items of stained glass for the Hartford house. But Twain, Livy told her mother, "suggested that I reserve it to pay the duties with, now wasn't that just like a man?"

THEY SAILED HOME from Europe in September 1879. Twain had seen a great deal more of the world than anyone in his family would have ever imagined, and from the vantage point of a well-traveled husband of an heiress, the Tennessee land he and his siblings had inherited seemed remote and insignificant. By this time, Twain had pretty much abandoned all hope of ever seeing any money from his father's investment in Tennessee real estate—and he no longer seemed to care. Even Orion was beginning to recognize that all his efforts had come to nothing. He had managed to sell some of the land, but in such small parcels and for such negligible prices that the profits scarcely paid the property taxes on whatever land remained.

Orion had a tough time determining just how much of it they still owned because titles were difficult to establish. "I am so sorry to hear you are cramped for means," he wrote to Pamela and their mother. It gave him "another twinge of conscience," he said, "that I fooled away the Tennessee land, and some of your money with it." Orion hadn't fooled it all away, it turns out, but there wasn't much left to get excited about.

IN THE SUMMER before their return from Europe, when Twain was thinking about illustrations for *A Tramp Abroad,* he told Frank Bliss, the son of Elisha Bliss, who took over the company upon his father's death, that he had come up with an image of his own that he wanted in the book. He had cut out a picture of a popular cartoon character and pasted it onto a "celebrated" Biblical scene. He wanted to attribute this comic mash-up to Titian. But to do justice to this masterpiece, they would need a master engraver to work on it—and he knew just the man. This fellow had been referred by Dan Slote, who, for reasons that are hard to imagine, was allowed to continue marketing Twain's scrapbook even after Slote's company had declared bankruptcy—and even after he had taken Twain's loan and sunk it into a company he knew was insolvent.

The engraver would use a new engraving process—"the best process in the world," Twain said—whose patent Slote had recently purchased. This new process was so promising, in fact, that in mid-February 1880, Slote sold Twain four-fifths of the patent for $5,000. Twain and Slote were in business together again, this time backing an invention that Twain told Orion "will utterly annihilate & sweep out of existence one of the minor industries of civilization, & take its place—an industry which has existed for 300 years." Maybe Twain was "mistaken in this calculation," he said, "but I am not able to see how I can be."

This innovation they called Kaolotype, a process for book illustration that involved the use of a clay mixture called kaolin and steel plates. Twain formed the Kaolotype Engraving Company, with himself as president and principal stockholder, and Slote as vice president and manager. Within two weeks of purchasing the stock, Twain had thought up new applications for the process that he told Orion would "increase the value of Kaolotype a hundred fold." It could also be used, Twain decided, for decorating book covers and for engraving type for their titles. But that meant somebody would have to invent something else—something that would enable bookbinders "to mould hard brass with sharp lines & perfect surfaces."

Twain did his usual due diligence. Which means he didn't do much at all, except meet with other visionaries like himself and one or two other thoroughly unscrupulous opportunists, and come away impressed with them all. Everybody who knew anything about the book business "laughed at the idea & said the thing was absolutely impossible." Everyone, that is, except a young German named Charles Sneider, an associate of Slote's and inventor of the Kaolotype process. Sneider believed he could do it, so Twain financed the perfection of the process. In November 1880, after months of work, Sneider and Slote showed up at Twain's house in Hartford with six examples of the brass stamps Sneider had been laboring on for use in the Kaolotype process.

Impressed with what he saw, Twain told Orion that Sneider "has worked the miracle." Delighted by the inventor's results, Twain put him on the payroll at $150 a month. He also built a workshop and headquarters building on Fulton Street, below

Union Square in Manhattan, where Sneider could continue his work, with Twain paying "attendant expenses." There was to be an additional $5,000 coming to Sneider when the new applications had been patented. "I never saw people so wild about anything," Twain told his brother.

Once Slote showed him some "handsome impressions" that Sneider had just produced, Twain decided to spend more than $20,000 for a piece of land adjacent to his own property, in order to build a greenhouse and to enlarge the mansion. A neighbor was planning to put up an outbuilding that would block Twain's view, so Twain walked to the lot, asked the man what he wanted for the land, and met his demand on the spot. "If the utility of our invention was *doubtful*," Twain told Slote, "I would allow my neighbor to go on digging his damned cellar, & build a house right in our faces."

Over the next year, Twain continued to invest even more sums in Slote and Sneider, all the while imagining still more applications for their process, "for wall-paper stamps, stamps for calico-printing, & stamps for embossed work on leather," he told Orion. Over time, however, Twain's confidence in Slote and Sneider, if not in the Kaolotype itself, began to give way to doubts. Slote wasn't the efficient manager that Twain had wanted, and in January 1881, Twain ordered Slote not to bother him with picayune decisions. "I started in to be a Figure-Head President & that's what I am."

More and more uneasy, Twain made an appointment to see for himself what his associates were up to. But there was a complication. The night before he was to visit the Fulton Street headquarters, it burned down. So he made another appointment, this time to visit Sneider's own workshop. It too burned down.

One such fire was plausible. Two raised serious suspicions.

Slote, meanwhile, was either unable to produce receipts for expenditures or simply refused to. To get to the bottom of things, Twain called in Charles Webster from Fredonia, New York, a village near Lake Erie. Webster was a twenty-two-year-old nephew by marriage "who seemed a capable and energetic young fellow." Webster was selling insurance in Fredonia when summoned to take over the Kaolotype business and various related ventures. In April 1881, Twain gave Webster complete authority over the day-to-day operations but also "started in at once to unload instructions, plans, and bright ideas onto his new helper." Within a week of Webster's involvement, he had looked at the company's books (such as they were), made inquiries, and turned up enough damaging information that Twain was ready not only to have Sneider fired, but arrested.

The samples Sneider claimed to have produced on the Kaolotype Engraving Company payroll, Webster discovered, had been produced before Twain had hired him. The contract with Sneider "was *based* on a lie & a fraud," Twain concluded. The $5,000 and the $150 a month salary, he told Webster,

> were to be paid for simply the two things—the delivery
> to us of *patents,* & the *development & perfecting* of a
> process already shown to have been accomplished. But it
> was all a lie, for Sneider had invented nothing new; he
> was working by old methods—& at the same time not
> succeeding with them. He pretended that the specimens
> he brought were made by the process described in the
> patents afterward issued to him, but such was not the
> case. It was exactly as if he had contracted to furnish me
> a process of making silver out of sawdust for a specific
> sum, & then claimed the sum on specimens of silver produced in the regular old time-honored way.

Twain wanted Sneider brought to justice "on a charge of obtaining money under false pretenses," and he wanted Slote to bear half the costs of bringing the charges. Slote, if anything, should "bear a larger proportion than that, because if he had stood to his part of the agreement & run the business himself, instead of taking Sneider's word for everything, the transparent swindle would have been detected long ago & the outlay stopped." Slote need not worry that they wouldn't prevail in court, because "the case is perfectly plain, & the penitentiary is perfectly sure."

But by now, Twain had grown as distrustful of Slote as he was of Sneider. Slote was still in charge of marketing the scrapbook, and here too he was falling short of the mark. Twain was being paid around $1,800 a year from scrapbook sales when he thought "it ought to have been 3 times as much." Slote, he decided, "took advantage of my utter confidence in his honesty to cheat me." Slote "knew he was lying . . . and also knew I was ass enough to believe him."

Webster pressed on with his investigations, and Twain offered suggestions. Twain wanted Webster to corner Sneider, then turn on Slote. But to build the case against Sneider, it might help to hint to Slote that he could "be proceeded against as a *party* to the swindle." Under pressure, Sneider cracked. "The bubble has burst," Webster told Twain in May 1881. Sneider "confessed [that] the whole thing was a swindle from the beginning," and was now threatening to kill himself. It's not clear whatever happened to Sneider, but there's no evidence that he was ever arrested or committed suicide. Slote died in February 1882. *Publishers' Weekly,* which ran an obituary, mentions no cause of death.

Had Slote died a year earlier, Twain said, "I should have been at the funeral, and squandered many tears; but as it is, I did not go and saved my tears." Under the protection of their friendship, Slote "stole from me for at least seven years . . . I came very near sending him to the penitentiary."

In one last effort to save the Kaolotype engraving process, Twain suggested that it be used for the images in *Life on the Mississippi,* published in May 1883. Wanting nothing to do with Sneider's so-called technological miracle, the illustrators refused. In his autobiography, Twain viewed the episode with rueful equanimity. He figured that with Slote in charge, he spent $500 a month just to keep the company going with nothing to show for it. "That raven flew out of the Ark regularly every thirty days," Twain wrote, "but it never got back with anything and the dove didn't report for duty." Webster was honest but, he decided, no more successful. He "continued to send the raven out monthly, with the same old result to a penny."

All told, Twain figured he lost $42,000 on the venture—or roughly $953,000 today—and eventually gave the patent away "to a man whom I long detested and whose family I desired to ruin. Then I looked around for other adventures." Twain was never at a loss for ideas, so Webster need not fret; Twain would include him in these adventures. There would be plenty for Webster to do, and his record to date was commendable.

Webster had even managed to wring some value out of the property in Tennessee. "I have some good news to tell you," Pamela wrote to Orion and his wife in May 1881. "Charley has sold the very last acre of Tennessee land. Is that not something to rejoice over?" Sold might be putting it too strongly. Pamela said he traded whatever was left of the land for a lot in St. Paul, Minnesota. Webster himself didn't know for sure if any acreage remained. No one did. But the family was eager to believe they had finally gotten some value from whatever was left of it.

Twain, who had come to dread any mention of "that hated property," refused to talk about it.

But Pamela was jubilant. The lot in St. Paul, she reported, had been assessed in 1880 for $800 or $850, and in 1881 for $1,050. So what if Webster sold the land when its value was increasing? They were rid of it at last. A city lot might not have been much, but it was something.

14

―――― ⌒ ――――

"The Proportions of My Prosperity"

Twain thought so well of Charley Webster's work he made him his business manager. This position entailed new responsibilities, not all of which would have been found in anyone's job description. Once, for example, Twain was convinced that the *New York Tribune* had a vendetta against him and was printing daily "insults, for two months on a stretch," and instructed Webster to scour the newspaper's files and send him copies of these affronts. Webster found nothing but a less-than-favorable review of *The Prince and the Pauper*.

Even Livy found chores for her husband's business manager. On more than one occasion she asked Webster to go to Burghart's furniture store in Manhattan to look at pieces she had chosen for the Hartford house. Eager to please, he would hustle back and forth to the store with a measuring stick to check on the dimensions of a dresser, and then, if it suited, approve the purchase and get it to Hartford by Christmas. After pestering him with one set of detailed instructions, she asked, with a trace of condescension, "Charley, do you understand all this?"

Webster did understand, evidently, for Twain soon gave him a promotion. In early 1884, dissatisfied with all of the other well-established publishers, Twain formed his own publishing house, Charles L. Webster & Company, Publishers, installing his nephew Charley as its titular head, chief sales agent, and office manager, with headquarters on the second floor of a building on Fulton Street in Manhattan. Twain's previous publishers, he decided, had fleeced him. He recalled his relationship with Elisha Bliss's American Publishing Company, which published *The Innocents Abroad* and other titles, as "ten years of swindlings." Bliss, he said, was a "skinny, yellow, toothless, bald-headed, rat-eyed professional liar and scoundrel [who] never did an honest thing in his life, when he had a chance to do a dishonest one." When Bliss died in 1880, Twain signed on with James R. Osgood and Company, which published *The Prince and the Pauper* in December 1881 and *Life on the Mississippi* in May 1883. Osgood, unlike Bliss, was "one of the dearest and sweetest human beings to be found on the planet anywhere." Unfortunately, Osgood knew "nothing about subscription publishing" and "made a mighty botch of it."

With Webster handling the day-to-day responsibilities (meaning when he was not running back and forth to measure dresser drawers at Burghart's), Twain thought he could do better, not only with publishing his own books, but with publishing those of other authors as well. By eliminating the middle man, Twain figured he could pocket the profits himself. Of course he would have to share earnings with Webster, which would require some negotiation. Twain was never completely convinced he should have been on salary at all. Webster was only learning his trade, after all, and Twain seems to have regarded him as a proto-intern. Brick masons weren't on salary when they were apprentices. Not even doctors and lawyers were salaried as apprentices. Twain wasn't salaried when he was a cub pilot on the Mississippi. He paid $500 to learn the river, and he had borrowed the down payment. A young man studying for the ministry told Twain that "even Noah got no salary for the first six months—partly on account of the weather and partly because he was learning navigation."

But then Twain looked at the situation in a different light. Maybe the very fact that Webster had dared to demand a salary said something about his unique gifts. With this possibility in mind, Twain decided that he had encountered in Webster "something entirely new to history." As such, he should not allow some other employer to snatch him up. Any young man

> starting life in New York without equipment of any kind, without proved value of any kind, without prospective value of any kind, yet able without blinking an eye to propose to learn a trade at another man's expense and charge for this benefaction an annual sum greater than any president of the United States had ever been able to save out of his pay for running the most difficult country on the planet, after Ireland, must surely be worth securing—and instantly—lest he get away.

So they came to terms. Webster was to receive $2,500 a year as well as a third of the first $20,000 of net profits, with a tenth of anything more than that. Twain would have to approve business expenses above $1,000, and, as Ron Powers puts it, he retained the right "to complain about the rest." And Twain did a good deal of complaining.

The first book scheduled for release by Charles L. Webster &

Company was *The Adventures of Huckleberry Finn*. Twain had been "fooling around" with the manuscript since at least 1876. In the summer of 1883, Twain retreated to Quarry Farm, where he hoped to finish it in just two months, but he kept getting distracted and his writing was forever being relegated to the back burner. By now, Webster knew all too well Twain's tendency to get derailed. The Kaolotype was hardly the only one of the side hustles that got in the way of Twain's work as a writer and publisher. There were, of course, his own inventions. "No one seems to have appreciated the fact that Mark Twain was an inventive genius. Except Mark Twain." That's how Samuel Webster, Charles Webster's son, put it in his book *Mark Twain, Business Man,* a spirited defense of his father's reputation against Twain's late-life attacks. Samuel Webster described the inventions as projects that Twain considered "greater than literature."

There was, for example, Mark Twain's Fact and Date Game, which, Samuel Webster said, "swept [Twain] off his feet." This was a board game that awarded points for a child's ability to recall events in English history, improving the player's memory in the process. Twain compiled extensive notes for the game and hired brother Orion to look up the names and dates to be used in it. During this period, the two brothers and both their households "thought of nothing else. *Huckleberry Finn* was quite forgotten."

But developing the game proved more difficult than Twain expected. He spent parts of more than twelve years trying to perfect it, more time than it took to write *Huckleberry Finn.* "If you haven't ever tried to invent an indoor historical game, don't," he told Howells. "I've got the thing at last so it will work, I guess, but I don't want any more tasks of that kind." At one point, Twain thought he had gotten the job done. In fact, he was only "entering the initiatory difficulties of it. I might have known it wouldn't be an easy job, or somebody would have invented a decent historical game long ago."

By August 1883, Twain felt the concept of the game was near enough to perfection to direct Webster to secure patents in the United States, Canada, and England. Meanwhile, Twain threw himself into the details of the game's construction—the design, for example, of cribbage-like game boards with pinholes punched in them and cloth inserted between the boards. "I think that several thicknesses of the commonest, coarsest, cheapest loose-woven blanketing or similar goods will answer our purpose quite well, when packed together pretty tightly between the boards—especially if we increase the depth a mere trifle, so as to give the pin a little deeper hold," he told Webster. "I don't believe an increased *depth* will be necessary, but we can do it *if* necessary." The following summer, "as soon as *Huck Finn* is published, you will go to work & publish one or two of the historical games—so be governed accordingly. There's bushels of dividends in those games."

But there weren't bushels or even brandy snifters of money in them. The game wasn't on the market until 1891, and the few stores to sell it did so only on consignment. People who tried to play the game found it too complicated even for adults—and much too tedious to be fun. One said it "looked like a cross between an income tax form and a table of logarithms." Considering the game's frigid reception, Twain told one of his office workers to "put it aside until some indefinite time in the far future—it isn't worth [the] trouble, now, when you can employ your time more profitably on other things. Besides, I am sorry I put my *name* to the Game; I wish I hadn't."

· · ·

ANOTHER DISTRACTION WAS the baby-bed clamp. The third of Twain's daughters, Jean Clemens, was born in 1880, so he was by now familiar with the tendency of infants to kick the sheets and covers off their beds and, supposedly, catch a cold as a result. This might not have caused much concern for most parents, but Twain evidently thought something should be done about it, and he was just the one to do it.

Twain envisioned a kind of clasp that would secure the bed sheets. But he then discovered in 1884 that a comparable device had already been patented and was being manufactured and marketed. So he bought out the company's interest in its product with the intention of substituting his own invention, which he felt was superior, anyway. He would also improve upon the other company's pricing, which he considered too cheap. This rival was selling its device for 90 cents when Twain thought it should be priced at $1.15.

With evident pride, Twain told Webster he had "invented a more expensive & more convenient one," thereby turning marketing wisdom on its head. Instead of undercutting the competition by offering a comparable product at a lower price, he would in fact charge more. By early 1885 he decided that at $1.15 the device was underpriced. "Even $2 is much too low for the bed-clamp," he said. "If I go into it eventually, it must be at $2.25 each for the small size, & $3 for the large."

Webster held his tongue only so long. After meeting with a possible manufacturer of the device, he sent along cost estimates and a recommendation. "You haven't asked my opinion," Webster said, "but I will say, I have no doubt that it will prove a failure. It is so entirely foreign to our business that I think it is unwise to go into it." He had "already heard of one case where it has been bought and paid for and thrown away as useless." Twain's response was to challenge the cost estimates. These figures, he thought, made no sense—at least to someone who didn't want to accept their implications.

"Try again," Twain said. "*Tabulate* the expenses of all kinds, in an intelligible way. And state some idea of what the *entire* expense will *be,* in dollars & cents; for '& expenses' means nothing." To comply with this request, Webster asked for more information. Twain refused. "No, it is business—so I don't want anything to do with it. You are there to take care of my business, not to make business for me to take care of."

Gradually Twain lost confidence in the commercial feasibility of the bed clamp, though as late as 1888, Webster was still afraid Twain might try to revive the idea. Samuel Webster also had firsthand experience with the baby-bed clamp. When he was an infant, his mother—Twain's niece—tested it on him. "I was used as the guinea pig for one of [Twain's] greatest inventions—a bed clamp to keep children from kicking off the covers," Webster writes. "But it didn't work so well in my case. There was nothing wrong with the bed-clamp—it was either the baby or the way it was hitched on. He probably suggested to my mother to get another baby."

Another salvo: "I might have an early prejudice against that bed-clamp, but I can't see the average young parent paying three dollars for it, even with [Twain's] improvements. Safety pins are much better and wouldn't tear the sheets any worse. Any fairly intelligent parent could have made one out of nearly anything." But Twain "had probably figured out how many babies were born every year and put down each one at $3 for his bed-clamp—or $2.25 at the lowest—and was getting rich off it. Why didn't he go into the chicken business?"

Finally: "Some people at this period had a wrong idea, that of making their products cheap so that people could buy them; but [Twain] rectified this false reasoning. An advantage of the bed clamp was that it kept Webster from frittering away time on the Grant book and *Huckleberry Finn*."

THERE WERE ALWAYS DISTRACTIONS. There was a perpetual calendar, which was some kind of a watch fob or charm that you could carry on your wrist and, no matter where you went, it never went out of date. No one really knows much about this invention, including museum curators, archivists, and Twain collectors. Twain referred to it only a few times in his correspondence and notebooks, and he never actually described it. In July 1884, for instance, he instructed Webster to "heave your surplus energies . . . [into] my soon-to-be patented portable calendar." But it appears from U.S. Patent Office records that the perpetual calendar was never patented.

There was also a "spiral pin" that Twain invented, which was supposed to keep ladies' hats from blowing off their heads in windy weather. He formed the International Spiral Pin Company to develop the invention and "put in ten or twelve thousand dollars," Twain wrote in 1904. But Twain never seemed to know much about the company and its operations because it "never makes an official report & also refrains from declaring dividends." Albert Bigelow Paine says Twain "had a number of the pins handsomely made to present to visitors of the sex naturally requiring that sort of adornment and protection. It was a pretty and ingenious device and apparently effective enough, though it failed to secure his invested thousands." At the time of Twain's death, he owned 133 shares in the company that were "believed to be worthless."

Then there was his adventure with the men he called the watch thieves. They were three brothers—one a jeweler, the other two patent medicine salesmen—in Fredonia. In 1881, using Webster's influence on his famous uncle, the brothers persuaded Twain to invest about $5,000 in the Independent Watch Company, which would later be known as the Fredonia Watch Company. Part of the agreement was that the company would produce and sell a Mark Twain pocket watch, "an early example of a celebrity-endorsed product, but unlike the George Foreman Grill or the Suzanne Somers ThighMaster of the subsequent century, the Mark Twain watch never generated any financial rewards for its namesake."

Upon discovering that the brothers were bilking what he called "confiding villagers"—himself included—Twain prepared an advertisement to run in newspapers as far away as Buffalo, threatening to expose the crooks. Webster seems to have shown the ad to the watch thieves, which worked. Twain got his money back, as well as that of his sister Pamela, who had invested, too. In the end, the company did manufacture the Mark Twain watch, and collectors still prize them.

THE GRANT BOOK, as Samuel Webster called it, was the second book issued by Twain's publishing firm. When Ulysses S. Grant and Twain met is a matter of dispute. Their encounter at a December 1879 army reunion in Grant's honor in Chicago was certainly not their first, since Twain said the former president would recall an earlier meeting. "He would remember me," Twain said, "because I was the person who did not ask him for an office." Twain also remembered suggesting back then that Grant write his memoirs.

Grant had put far too much trust in political cronies during his scandal-ridden presidency, and after leaving the White House, he invested heavily in a brokerage firm that collapsed as a result of a business partner's dishonesty. Credulity, to Twain, was nothing to be ashamed of. He could be guilty of it himself. Besides, Twain genuinely liked and admired Grant, and when he heard that his Civil War memoirs were in the works, he wanted them for Charles L. Webster & Company.

Unfortunately, Grant had promised them in a handshake deal to the Century Company, publisher of *Century* magazine. The magazine, which had run some of Grant's battlefield recollections, decided to expand them into a book. The Century Company offered 10 percent royalties with no advance, with what Twain called an "offensive" detail. Part of the 10 percent would be withheld for "sweeping out the offices, or some such nonsense as that."

In late 1884, a few days after learning of Century's offer, Twain called on Grant at his Manhattan residence. There he told Grant that the deal the publisher had proposed underestimated the book's "commercial magnitude." The terms "indicate that they expect it to sell five, possibly ten thousand copies. A book from your hand, telling the story of your life and battles, should sell not less than a quarter of a million, perhaps twice that sum. It should be sold only by subscription, and you are entitled to double the royalty here proposed. I do not believe it is to your interest to conclude this contract without careful thought and investigation."

Grant was unconvinced. While he had signed no contract, he still felt honor-bound to give the book to the publisher that first suggested it.

"General, if that is so," Twain said, "it belongs to *me.*"

He then reminded Grant that he had urged him to write his memoirs years before—and that he should allow Twain to take charge of its publication.

"General," he went on, "I am publishing my own book and by the time yours is ready it is quite possible that I shall have the best equipped subscription establishment in the country. If you place your book with my firm—and I feel that I have at least an equal right in the consideration—I will pay you twenty per cent of the list price, or, if you prefer, I will give you seventy per cent of the net returns and I will pay all office expenses out of my thirty per cent." Twain would pay for "sweeping out the offices" himself.

Grant, who would soon be diagnosed with throat cancer, signed a contract with Webster & Company in February 1885. Over the next few months, Grant worked on the manuscript, soldiering on even as he became increasingly frail and in pain and, toward the end, unable to speak. In the summer, when the manuscript was complete, he died, and Twain's often harried staff at Webster & Company pushed the book toward publication. Volume one of *The Personal Memoirs of Ulysses S. Grant* was released in December. Sales exceeded everyone's expectations—except Twain's. In February of 1886, Julia Dent Grant, the author's widow, was presented with a check for $200,000, roughly the equivalent today of $4 million, and, at its time, the largest single royalty payment ever made. The second volume was published in March of that year. More than 300,000 sets of the two volumes were sold, and Charles L. Webster & Company paid Grant's widow more than $400,000, or about $8 million in today's currency. Twain earned about $200,000 from the venture.

Webster & Company had another brisk seller on its hands, too. *Huckleberry Finn* was released in the United States in February 1885, the same month that Grant signed his contract with the firm. When *Huckleberry Finn* sold out its initial run of 30,000 copies, Webster & Company rushed out another 10,000 in March. When the public library in Concord, Massachusetts, announced later in the month that it wouldn't lend the ill-bred Huck's story to its genteel patrons, Twain immediately recognized the value of what we call "buzz." The library has "given us a rattling tip-top puff which will go into every paper in the country," he told Webster, immediately generating 25,000 more sales. As we know today, there's never been a time when the novel wasn't controversial, and there has never been a time when it was out of print. At last count, *Huckleberry Finn* had sold at least 20 million copies in no fewer than fifty languages.

With the booming profits from *Huckleberry Finn* and Grant's memoir, Twain told Howells he was "totally free from debt." Twain, who would soon turn fifty, had achieved an astonishing level of fame; he claimed to be "frightened by the proportions of my prosperity. It seems that whatever I touch turns to gold." Aflame with confidence, Twain was now eager to exercise his Midas touch and grow that fortune.

15

"This Awful Mechanical Miracle"

The next enterprise to which the Midas touch was to be applied was one Twain actually knew something about. He first learned of this new investment opportunity a few years earlier, when the owner of a jewelry store on Hartford's Main Street came to call. The two men met in Twain's billiard room, "which was my study," though billiards always "got more study than the other sciences." The jeweler told Twain that an inventor he knew, one James W. Paige, was working on a machine that would revolutionize the newspaper business. Paige, who rented a workshop at the Colt Armory, was about finished with the prototype. He was looking for investors. Twain could get in on the ground floor.

It was a machine for setting type. Twain, though skeptical, was nonetheless intrigued. Type was set the same way in the 1880s as it had been when Twain worked as a printer's devil thirty years earlier—by hand. In fact, typesetting hadn't changed much since Ben Franklin's day, or even Gutenberg's. Newspaper proprietors were eager to find a way to perform the costly, labor-intensive function by machine, and in the 1870s a number of tinkerers were at work to meet the demand. Twain recognized the need to find a cheaper, more efficient, and less error-prone method for setting type, but he also had real-world, hands-on understanding of how difficult it would be to accomplish this goal.

This skepticism was also rooted in his suspicion that the wonders Paige's machine was supposed to perform would not be possible until other technological innovations had first been achieved—technological innovations he could not himself imagine and spoke of with some amusement. "I knew all about typesetting by practical experience," Twain said, "and held [with] the settled and solidified opinion that a successful typesetting machine was an impossibility, for the reason that a machine cannot be made to *think*, and the thing that sets movable type must think of retiring defeated." But Twain was willing to take a flier on the possibility that this prejudice of his might be unwarranted. He was "always taking little chances like that; and almost always losing by it, too—a thing which I did not greatly mind, because I was always careful to risk only such amounts as I could easily afford to lose."

WHEN TWAIN MET PAIGE and saw Paige's work in progress, he was greatly impressed. He went to the Colt Armory, "promising myself nothing," but came away eager to invest. Paige himself was impressive. He was "bright-eyed, alert, smartly dressed," and a great salesman and presenter. He "could persuade a fish to come out and take a walk with him."

The Paige Compositor, as it was called, might not have been able to think, but it seemed to behave almost as if it could. It was unquestionably a marvel of complexity. The patent application included 275 sheets of drawings and 123 more of specifications. The 5,000-pound contraption had more than 18,000 parts, with a 109-key keyboard worked by only one man. Pieces of type were dropped from upright silos, each of which held 200 characters. Dropped from its silo, the type slid into what has been described as a "raceway," in which the lines of type were assembled. Once the type was used, it was dumped underneath, where it would be shuttled back up to the top and deposited into the appropriate silo. The only thing the Paige Compositor couldn't do (besides write newspaper stories itself) was make sure the lines ran flush right, or were, as they say, "justified." An assistant had to insert steel spaces of various sizes to make the lines come out even at the end.

When the machine worked, it set type six times faster than a skilled human typesetter could. Using a Paige machine, Twain said, a New York daily could set up an entire page for what it "now costs to set a column by hand." It had additional advantages, too. The Paige Compositor "does not get drunk," and it "does not join the Printer's Union."

There were, by Twain's reckoning, 11,000 newspapers and periodicals being published. If only 1,000 of their publishers installed a Paige Compositor, he figured revenues would reach $2.5 million. Twain was not insensitive to the fact that this technological innovation would make many jobs obsolete. Economist Joseph Schumpeter, author of *Capitalism, Socialism and Democracy,* called it "creative destruction." Innovation always costs a lot of people their jobs, but Twain contented himself — as champions of innovation always do — by claiming it would actually create jobs, given time. As newspaper production costs declined, more and bigger newspapers would be printed. Higher profits would allow publishers to reinvest their profits into their businesses, producing more printed materials. For every typesetter who lost his job, Twain said, "10 will *get* work."

This very question—the effect of technological innovation on the newspaper business—was not entirely new. The French economist Frederic Bastiat addressed it, and his view seems to align well with Twain's, though there is no evidence Twain ever read Bastiat or, for that matter, any other economist. Even in Bastiat's day (he died in 1850) the price of producing newspapers had fallen, saving money not only for publishers but also for subscribers. But this savings didn't mean newspaper subscribers would simply subscribe to more newspapers, or that more newspapers would be published, as Twain argued. Even if consumers did not subscribe to more newspapers and more newspapers were not published, Bastiat said the savings would be invested somewhere else. Maybe some consumers might use the money saved to subscribe to more newspapers, but that didn't really matter, because others would use it to buy new clothes and yet others would buy better furniture.

"It is thus," Bastiat wrote, "that the trades are bound together. They form a vast whole, whose different parts communicate by secret channels; what is saved by one, profits all."

That was Twain's view, and the view of countless entrepreneurs today. Innovation benefits all mankind, and especially the man who can monetize it.

Twain invested $2,000 in Paige's machine almost immediately. After seeing the machine and meeting its inventor, he invested $3,000 more. Twain invested yet again and waited while the inventor kept working out the bugs. Before long, Twain was bankrolling the inventor and his machine to the tune of $3,000 per month. He had not laid eyes on Paige for at least a year when, one day in late 1885, the inventor showed up unannounced at the Hartford house. He told Twain the machine was almost perfect—that it would soon be able to justify the lines—but he needed more money.

"What will it cost?" Twain asked.

"$20,000," Paige said. "Certainly not over $30,000."

Twain, who was "flush" at the time, said, "I'll do it, but the limit must be $30,000."

Under the new contract, Twain assumed full responsibility for finding additional financing and for marketing the compositor. Frank Whitmore, a neighbor and insurance man who was put on Twain's payroll to oversee Paige, warned Twain not to sign the new agreement, which could make Twain almost solely responsible for the entire venture, especially because it could become ruinously expensive. That contract, Whitmore said, "can bankrupt you."

"I've considered that," Twain said. "I can get a thousand men worth a million apiece to go in with me if I can get a perfect machine."

Even Albert Bigelow Paine, in his wholly sympathetic biography, described the euphoria that gripped Twain during this period as almost beyond imagining. Notebook pages were filled with the angel investor's calculations—and with lists of prospective investors and how much capital they would be likely to invest. Twain figured 2,173 typesetters would be needed in the United States alone, with 6,500 worldwide. Twain "began to calculate the number of millions he would be worth" when the machine "was completed and announced to a waiting world." His figures "never ran short of millions, and frequently approached the billion mark." He said it "would take ten men to count the profits from the typesetter."

But within a year, the $30,000 had been spent, and Paige had still not "perfected" the machine. He now needed $4,000 more to finish his work, and for an extra $10,000, he could demonstrate it at an exhibition in New York. In effect, he had started over. He was working on a completely new machine, this time at the Pratt & Whitney factory in Hartford. The Paige 2.0 would require 20,000 parts—compared to "only" 18,000 before. Undaunted, Twain gave the inventor $4,000 more, and then kept advancing him more money until he was spending up to $4,000 a month. In early 1888, he had invested some $80,000 —or $1,950,000 in our time—in the venture, and seemed not a great deal closer to putting the compositor on the market.

At first, the time it was taking to get the machine ready did not concern Twain unduly; but later, of course, as the money he was sinking into the compositor drained his accounts, he began to worry about the delays—and about Paige himself. As enraptured as he was with inventors and inventions, he also understood that great inventions are not, in fact, the work of one isolated genius, barricaded for years in his dimly lit basement. They are in large part the result of communities of diligent amateurs who follow each other's progress—sometimes by reading trade journals, sometimes by knowing one another and discussing the challenges they face.

Technological breakthroughs are also the result of the accumulated knowledge of entire societies. Understanding all this provided Twain some comfort as he watched and waited—and continued to invest in the Paige Compositor. "It takes a thousand men to invent a telegraph, or a steam engine, or a phonograph, or a photograph, or a telephone or any other important thing—and the last man gets the credit and we forget the others," he said. The actual inventor "added his little mite—that is all he did. These object lessons should teach us that ninety-nine parts of all things that proceed from the intellect are plagiarisms, pure and simple; and the lesson ought to make us modest. But nothing can do that."

AS PAIGE TINKERED with his compositor, inventors were already marketing less complicated machines, with Ottmar Mergenthaler's Linotype machine enjoying the first-mover advantage. *New York Sun* publisher William Laffan, who had seen a demonstration of the Mergenthaler, told Twain he should be wary of this competition, which every New York daily will be using "inside of twelve months." Twain shrugged off this warning. He was "unaffrighted" of the Mergenthaler—and of all the other Mergenthalers of the world. By 1887, Laffan was still impressed with the Mergenthaler Linotype and told Twain the New York newspaper publishers were "all ready to talk machines." Still unaffrighted, Twain said it would take 157 Mergenthalers to set the type for the 419 pages that all the New York papers published each week, but only 63 Paige Compositors.

Yet the Paige Compositor was still not done, and the *New York Tribune* had already ordered twenty-three Mergenthalers. Irony of ironies, Twain had had the chance to invest in Mergenthaler's machine—its investors had offered the Paige investors a trade of stock in each other's companies—but Twain had declined. The fact that Mergenthaler's investors had wanted a piece of the Paige Compositor only convinced him of its superiority.

But Twain's confidence and his family's financial resources were not inexhaustible. He was now starting to lose faith in Paige and began to fear that Whitmore's prediction might prove true. Finally, in January 1888, Paige said his machine would be ready by April 1. On April 1, he said September. Then September came and went, and in October, he said he had three more months of work to do. "The machine is apparently almost done," Twain told Orion in November, "but I take no privileges on that account; it must be done before I spend a cent that can be avoided. I have kept this family on short commons for two years and they must go on scrimping until the machine is finished, no matter how long that may be."

"Scrimping," of course, must be seen in the context of the society in which Twain moved. The family still inhabited its mansion, where they were waited on by servants. The girls still had private tutors and took music and dancing lessons. But Livy, who was now forty, was having to keep a close eye on the finances. She had rarely had to do so earlier in her married life and looked forward to the day when she could again relax about money and follow her own generous impulses to her family, to friends, to servants, and to the needy of Hartford. Each Christmas, she prepared and distributed 110 food baskets, and she wondered sometimes how long she could continue to do so. "How strange it will seem," Livy wrote, "to have unlimited means, to be able to do whatever you want to do, to give whatever you want to give without counting the cost."

Just two years earlier, Twain had been "frightened at the proportions of my prosperity." Now, after investing so heavily in the typesetting machine, he needed money but was too distracted by business to write the books that could have been his bread and butter. He was working on *A Connecticut Yankee in King Arthur's Court* in early 1886, but by November he hadn't made the progress he had hoped to make. "Only two or three chapters have been written, thus far," he told a friend. "I expect to write three chapters a year for thirty years; then the book will be done."

Their vacation that year was not to Europe, but to Iowa. They went to Keokuk to see Twain's mother, who was living with Orion and his wife. Twain was aware that he was now on the other side of fifty and that less than a year before, he had been rich—really rich. But he sensed that unless the profits he envisioned from the typesetting machine were in fact realized, they might live out the rest of their days in poverty, albeit of the genteel variety. Despite early successes with *Huckleberry Finn* and Grant's memoir, there was no guarantee that these profitable books would be followed by others of comparable commercial appeal. The pressure was on, and Twain was growing impatient with Paige and his endless dithering.

Twain, meanwhile, redoubled his efforts to raise additional capital. He contacted the big-hearted John Percival Jones, invited him to Hartford, and entertained him at the mansion. He told Jones that from American newspapers alone the Paige Compositor would earn $35 million a year, and another $20 million from Europe. Then he took Jones to see a demonstration of the machine. But when they arrived at the Pratt & Whitney factory, there was a hitch. A day or two before their visit, Paige had decided to add a feature—an "air blaster"—so the machine Jones had come to see firsthand had been disassembled. Underwhelmed, Jones left.

The air blaster—whatever it did—was considered an improvement. A machine that could also justify lines was not only improved, it was perfected—and Paige was nothing if not a perfectionist. Paige again talked his benefactor into the pursuit of perfection. "What a talker he is!" Twain said. "When he is present, I always believe him; I can't help it." So it was back to the drawing board yet again.

Then, finally, just after New Year's there was a break. Twain, four other men, and the inventor gathered at the Pratt & Whitney factory for a demonstration of the machine in its latest iteration. Afterward, Twain wrote in his notebook:

> *EUREKA!*
>
> Saturday, January 5, 1889 — 12:20 p.m. At this moment I have seen a line of movable type *spaced and justified* by machinery! This is the first time in the history of the world that this amazing thing has ever been done.

Then he shared the glad tidings. "This is by far and away the most marvelous invention ever contrived by man," he told a London publisher. "And it is not a thing of rags and patches; it is made of massive steel, and will last a century." The "death-warrant of all other type-setting machines in this world was signed at 12:20 this afternoon." Twain was no less enthusiastic in telling Orion the news:

> All the other wonderful inventions of the human brain sink pretty nearly into commonplaces contrasted with this awful mechanical miracle. Telephones, telegraphs, locomotives, cotton-gins, sewing machines, Babbage calculators, Jacquard looms, perfecting presses, all mere toys, simplicities! The Paige Compositor marches alone and far into the land of human inventions.

Or so it seemed.

16

"Our Prosperity Became Embarrassing"

There were other projects on Twain's agenda during this period besides the Paige Compositor, of course. On the publishing front, the week after *Huckleberry Finn* sold out and Grant's widow received her royalty checks, Twain dispatched Charley Webster to Rome. There Webster was to go over details of the firm's next big book deal. This was to be an authorized biography of Pope Leo XIII, which was already being written by Father Bernard O'Reilly, the author of, among other books, *The Mirror of True Womanhood*.

The rights to the pope's book were apparently owned by Charles Dana of the *New York Sun*. Twain sent Webster to offer Dana $100,000 to buy the rights. Evidently, Dana took the money, because, in 1886, Twain's company signed a contract with Vatican officials and took over the project. Webster's assignment in Rome was to make sure all parties to the new contract fully understood its terms. Minor details still had to be worked out, like how much access the author and publisher would have to the Holy Father, and what degree of control his Holiness would have over the book.

Twain couldn't have been more excited. The target market was immense, and the book's sales would make those of Grant's memoir seem paltry and insignificant. When he discussed the book with Howells, Twain spoke

> in a sort of delirious exultation. He had no words in which to paint the magnificence of the project, or to forecast its colossal success. It would have a currency bounded only by the number of Catholics in Christendom. It would be translated into every language which was anywhere written or printed; it would be circulated literally in every country of the globe, and [Twain's] book agents would carry the prospectuses and then the bound copies of the work to the ends of the whole earth. Not only would every Catholic buy it, but every Catholic must, as he was a good Catholic, as he hoped to be saved.

Webster was to enjoy a private audience with the pope, and Twain was determined to send a suitable present for the Holy Father. Twain envisioned a special edition of Grant's memoir, with a calfskin binding and solid gold lettering, designed and engraved by Tiffany. The gold alone, Twain told Webster, would weigh "a couple of pounds, perhaps, & cost $500." He was willing to spend up to $12,000 on this special edition of the book, for the publicity value would be tremendous. It would be on display in Tiffany's window, and "all New York & all strangers visiting New York would flock to see it." Newspapers would publish pictures of the book, "& descriptions of it would appear in all languages & in all the newspapers in the world—&

Webster & Co. would score another point in the way of originality & enterprise."

To the letter in which Twain presented these ideas, he affixed a PS. The gold, he figured, "would cost nearer $3,000, instead of $500. That is all the better. And so I still think the idea is sound. Can't get so much advertising so cheaply in any other way."

But the gold-plated edition of the *Memoirs* proved too costly or otherwise impractical, and Webster sailed for Europe bearing a more modest version of the Grant book. Even so, Webster's visit to Rome did not lack for grandeur. In July 1886, he was taken to the Vatican in a carriage, with a plumed footman at his service. There, gazing on the white-haired man on a gilt throne, Webster discussed the book with the pope. The pope proved surprisingly well informed about the American book business. He knew how many copies of Grant's memoir had been sold, for example, and seemed impressed when told that his own life story was guaranteed to sell at least 100,000 copies. Whatever other matters they discussed aren't known, but everyone seemed delighted with how well the meeting went. "You did well to go to Rome, & you did wisely to spend money freely," Twain told Webster.

Livy was happy for Webster but envious too. "Ah," she said, "why didn't we go, too?"

THE POPE GOT his copy of Grant's memoir, and Webster, though not a Catholic himself, received a papal knighthood. As a "proof of Pontifical consideration," he was made a Knight of the Order of Pius. Deeply moved, Webster ordered (from France) a Knight of Pius uniform. This, according to the bill of sale, consisted of a

coat of bleu stuff lined of silk with revolts & neck of
scarlat stuff embroidered with fine gold, fine gilded but-
tons with the coat of arms of the Pope. Pants of fine
white cashemir with bands of fine gold. Epaulettes of fine
gold in granes [*sic*] with a star embroidered with silver.
Sword-holder of white stuff, little sword with gilded hilt
with mother of pearl, dragon of fine gold, pointed hat
embroidered with gold & little flakes of cocarde of the
Pope. Rosette & mostrine included for the black dress.

It was, in other words, just the thing for an American book
publisher to wear to the office. Maybe not on casual Friday, but
certainly every other day of the week. Webster's son remembered seeing his father wear the uniform once or twice in Fredonia, where the local newspaper took to calling him Sir Charles
Webster. "We were very short of foreign titles in Fredonia," he
explained. In Fredonia, he said, the druggist's son was always
called "Doc."

Twain was only a little put off by Webster's high honor. If
the pope made Webster a knight, Twain said, he ought to have
made him an archangel. He could get on well with people from
almost all stations in life, but Twain wasn't especially interested
in meeting a pope. He would prefer "to swap courtesies with
the cardinals and archbishops," who "are nearer my size."

Of course, Twain did not come away from Webster's papal
audience exactly empty-handed. Webster gave his boss's family
a rosary blessed by the pope. Neither Twain nor Livy nor their
daughters were Catholics, but they were thrilled with the present. The pope's rosary created such a "stir in this household as
was before utterly unimaginable," Twain wrote to Webster's
wife. "I would not take a thousand dollars for it — & I guess
your aunt Livy's price would run higher still. We have three ex-

cellent girls in the house, & I believe they value more the telling their beads on that rosary than they would the handling [of] government bonds that fell in their laps as a free gift."

Livy so cherished the rosary that she expressed a desire "to send some money to Father O'Reilly to buy three more with, & see if [Charley] can't persuade him to get the Holy Father to bless them. If Charley thinks it would be an indelicate or improper thing to ask, he mustn't think about it any further; but otherwise Livy would very much like it." She wanted to present them to three of the family's Irish servants.

WHILE ALL THESE FORMALITIES were playing out, O'Reilly finished the manuscript, and Twain oversaw design of the brochure for sales agents to distribute on their rounds. This, the brochure proclaimed, was "The Greatest Book of the Age," issued in six languages, with the price kept low enough that every household could afford its own copy. Everything was falling into place. Aided by the sales brochure, the book was "going to *go*, sure."

Except it didn't go. Published in 1887, *The Life of Pope Leo XIII* fell far short of the promised 100,000 copies. Howells, who had been nearly as charged up as Twain by the book's prospects, realized the flaw in their calculations. "We did not consider how often Catholics could not read, how often when they could, they might not wish to read. The event proved that whether they could read or not the immeasurable majority did not wish to read the life of the Pope," even though it was "issued to the world with every sanction of the Vatican."

It was all a little like the baby-bed clamp. Yes, there were multitudes of people who had babies—millions of them—but that didn't mean they all wanted to buy a baby-bed clamp. Yes, there were Catholics all over the world, but that didn't mean all of them wanted to read, much less buy, this book. The intended purchaser, Paine wrote, "had decided that the Pope's *Life* was not necessary to his salvation or even to his entertainment."

There was another problem that Twain and Howells never seemed to notice. Leo XIII had been pope for only nine years when Webster & Company published his autobiography. His papacy was just getting started; it did not end until his death in 1903. Leo XIII was the oldest pope and ultimately had the third-longest pontificate. People might have wanted to read about his papacy once there had been more of it, but at this early stage there wasn't much of a story to tell. Later on, there would be. Even non-Catholics might like to read about how he was the first pope to allow himself to be filmed by a motion picture camera. (Afterward, he blessed the camera.)

The book's failure hit Twain hard. This was almost incomprehensible to him. His "sanguine soul was utterly confounded," Howells recalled, "and soon a silence fell upon it where it had been so exuberantly jubilant."

At the same time that Webster & Company was struggling with the pope's biography, its other sure-fire hit was the life story of another major religious figure of the age. This was Henry Ward Beecher, one of the most famous, most beloved, and most controversial Americans of his time. The pastor of Brooklyn's Plymouth Congregational Church, Beecher associated himself with the most advanced enthusiasms of the century: abolition, female suffrage, Darwinian evolution, and phrenology, which purported to discern a person's psychological makeup from the bumps on the subject's head. Beecher was also an impassioned advocate of welcoming Chinese immigrants. He said they could do "what we call menial work."

Twain's and Beecher's paths had crossed—sort of—with

the *Quaker City* cruise. Beecher was to be the most illustrious passenger. His name was used as advertising to attract other pilgrims. When he decided not to go on the cruise, forty customers also dropped out. Beecher was also the brother of Twain's neighbor Harriet Beecher Stowe and a frequent visitor to Hartford. In early 1887, when Beecher pondered writing his life story, he thought Webster & Company should publish it. "I do not love Beecher any more than you do," Webster told Twain, "but I love his money just as well, and I am certain that book would sell."

There were good reasons for this optimism. Not only was Beecher a household name, he'd become one, in part, because he had been the defendant in one of the most sensational courtroom dramas of the decade, if not the century. In 1875, while using his pulpit to preach against Free Love, he was practicing it in private, with a parishioner. A few years earlier, a woman in his congregation told her husband she had been carrying on an affair with Beecher. The cuckolded husband then told Elizabeth Cady Stanton, who in turn passed along this juicy bit of gossip to Victoria Woodhull, the outspoken stockbroker, spiritualist, and 1872 presidential candidate on the Equal Rights Party ticket. Woodhull published an account of the affair in her weekly newspaper.

Beecher's indignant response was to call on the police to arrest Woodhull on obscenity charges, which they did. Plymouth Church excommunicated Beecher's mistress's husband, who then sued Beecher for alienation of affection. The case went to trial. Twain and Joseph Twichell, his Hartford pastor, were among the spectators in the courtroom. After six days of deliberation, the trial ended with a hung jury. Beecher asked the Congregational church to conduct its own investigation, which it did—and exonerated him. (Rumors of similar infidelities dogged Beecher's entire career. "Beecher," it was said, "preaches to seven or eight of his mistresses every Sunday evening.")

Twain saw a gold mine in Beecher's story, and in January 1887 signed him to a book deal with a $5,000 advance. Within a month of the signing, Twain said his valuation of the book had gone up already, presumably based on what he had since seen of Beecher's work in progress. "If he writes the book in that way, & heaves in just enough piousness," Twain told Webster, the profits would hit $350,000. Twain later upped that figure to $750,000 — or, in today's currency, roughly $18 million.

But things never seemed to work out quite as Twain planned, did they? On March 8, 1887, just weeks after the contract was signed, Beecher died, not of shame, apparently, but from a stroke. Loss of the $5,000 advance was easily absorbed. But in preparing for publication of the autobiography, Webster & Company had begun to purchase paper and other materials. By the time of Beecher's death, the firm had already spent $100,000 on those supplies.

THEN THERE WAS another hitch in the operations of Webster & Company. In the summer of 1885, Webster became suspicious of Frank Scott, the company's bookkeeper and cashier. Some unsigned letters sent to company higher-ups claimed Scott was a thief. Webster was also aware that Scott had begun to speculate on Wall Street. Webster alerted Twain to his suspicions and told him that he intended to trap the scoundrel. Webster seemed almost too eager to do so, as it offered him "a chance to play detective," Twain said, "and snoop and spy around and catch somebody committing sin." Webster "was very fond of detective work" and seems to have seen himself "about on a level with Sherlock Holmes."

Webster's plan was "to pass some marked banknotes through

his hands and see if they would stick," but this proved unnecessary. Fred Grant, the general's son and a member of Webster &
Company's board, lost patience with the way the company was
handling the investigation and showed up unannounced one
day with his own team of accountants. When they began going
over the ledgers, the "color went out of poor Scott's face, and he
looked very sick," Twain said. "He excused himself from further attendance—said he would go home and lie down."

Webster's suspicions were well founded. Scott had made off
with $25,000—or $611,000 these days. In March 1887, he
turned himself in, confessed to the crime, and was sentenced in
April to six years' hard labor at the New York penitentiary at
Sing Sing. Now it was Twain's turn to engage in a little detective
work. He instructed Webster to hire detectives to find out where
Scott had hidden the money and to get it back. He surely
couldn't have spent it all. If the detectives couldn't locate the
missing greenbacks, Webster was to dispose of all of Scott's personal property, including the house he was building in Roseville, New Jersey, "the finest suburb of Newark." The house was
sold in November. There's no evidence Twain ever hired any
detectives or found any greenbacks under the floorboards, but
somehow the company successfully recovered about $8,000 of
the missing $25,000.

Three years later, Twain and Webster petitioned New York
Governor David Hill for Scott's pardon. After Scott had served
more than half of his sentence, Twain and Webster again petitioned the governor, this time for the embezzler's release so he
could support his wife and children. Scott's sentence was commuted in late December 1890 to time served.

For some reason Twain seems to have taken pity on Scott,
but not on Webster. If his nephew had been a more hands-on
supervisor, Twain decided, Scott's thievery would have been de-

tected much earlier, at less of a loss to the company. Ideally, Scott would never have been hired at all. A competent background check—the kind conducted by HR departments today—would have eliminated the man from consideration. "It was easy to trace him from employment to employment," Twain wrote. "In fact you could trace him from one employment to the next by the stolen money which he had dripped along the road."

Webster & Company was now struggling, even without Scott's embezzlement. The firm was never able to duplicate the success of Grant's memoir. Not for lack of trying, though. It published *McClellan's Own Story* by George McClellan, *Personal Memoirs of P. H. Sheridan,* and *Memoirs of Gen. W. T. Sherman.* In 1888, Frederick J. Hall, who was hired as a stenographer at the firm and who would ultimately replace Webster when his health broke down, returned from meetings with sales agents with bad news. "War literature of any kind and no matter by whom written is played out," Hall told Twain. There was "not a man today who could write another book on the war and sell 5,000 in the whole country." (In fact, the whole subscription book business model was becoming obsolete. The use of sales agents made for high overhead, and more small towns now had bookstores. In time, Webster & Company abandoned the subscription model altogether.)

Among other poor decisions, Twain insisted on publishing a book of sermons by the Reverend Nathaniel J. Burton, a Hartford neighbor, even though Webster tried to talk him out of it. Webster's son remembered that dispute with rueful amusement. "Probably everybody on the block would have bought the book," Samuel Webster wrote. "Or borrowed it." Other titles weren't much more promising. *The Biography of Ephraim*

McDowell, M.D. ("Father of Ovariotomy"); *One Hundred Ways of Cooking Eggs; A Perplexed Philosopher: Being an Examination of Mr. Herbert Spencer's Various Utterances on the Land Question;* and *The Speech of Monkeys, in Two Parts* seem not to have excited the farmers and their wives when sales agents called. (It's not clear what the sales figures were for another Webster book, William Schmidt's *The Flowing Bowl: What and When to Drink,* but it probably got well used around the office.)

A color catalog of William Thompson Walters's collection of Old Masters' paintings, which Twain said would be "infinitely grander & finer than any ever issued in any country in the world," was to bring in $700,000 or $800,000 in profits. Twain said there was "reputation in it for us—and cash." He called it a "greenback-mine." Webster & Company never issued the book, although a version was published in 1897, three years after Twain's firm ceased operations.

While some of the publisher's books sold well, such as Twain's *A Connecticut Yankee in King Arthur's Court,* these earnings could hardly cover the costs of all the titles that sold poorly. The most prestigious offering was a massive eleven-volume *Library of American Literature,* which included material from 1,200 other authors, including Hawthorne, Longfellow, and Melville. There were more than 2,600 selections and over 300 full-page illustrations, the whole kit and caboodle to be sold on the subscription model. Richard Zacks, in *Chasing the Last Laugh,* does an admirable job summing up the project's flaw.

> Customers had to pay only the first $3 monthly install-
> ment of the $33 cover price to receive the entire set, but
> it cost the company $13 to print, bind and ship, and an-

other $12 in commission to the agents. The publisher
was $22 in the red on every sale, and, as the economy
soured, customers increasingly stopped paying install-
ments. Delinquent payments ballooned from $28,862 in
1891 to $67,795 in 1892.

Fred Hall, Webster's assistant, explained the problem this
way: "The faster installment orders came in, the faster our capital shrank, until our prosperity became embarrassing." Finally,
there wasn't much gain for the company even in the books that
were profitable in the near term, and for this reason: Twain had
insisted on pumping profits from the publishing company into
the Paige Compositor operation, while the inventor continued
to pursue its perfection. This business model, as we'd say today,
was not sustainable.

The daily pressure of operating under these extremely stress-
ful conditions eventually took its toll on Webster. First, there
was a nagging cough, then nerve pain. "I am not whining," he
wrote, "but I have actually ruined my health by the hard work
I did two years ago" on Grant's memoir. As early as the summer
of 1887, Webster was suffering from symptoms of neuralgia.
His mental state was deteriorating rapidly, partly from the
stress of working for such a demanding and capricious boss
who seemed incapable of focusing on the core business of book
publishing. Webster was becoming increasingly irritable, and
"the slightest thing would bring an outburst," his son recalled.

Webster could come to the office only sporadically and admitted he was no longer able to earn his salary. In February
1888, after he had what his son called a breakdown, he was
convinced to retire and sold his share in the publishing company for $12,000. "How long he has been a lunatic I do not
know," Twain said, but he too traced it to the year they were

gearing up to release the Grant book. Twain was never able to admit (or maybe recognize) that he could be a difficult employer, but even he admitted to Webster that it had been "an exceedingly hard summer" for him.

Webster was only in his midthirties when he left the company and returned to Fredonia. There he opened a museum of some kind in his house and built a cupola with a revolving top equipped with a telescope. He was just thirty-nine when he died in April of 1891, after what a newspaper obituary described as "an attack of grip, which led to peritonitis and hemorrhage, and caused death." On his tombstone he wanted the words, "Publisher of Gen. Grant's Memoirs & Knighted by the Pope." As it turned out, Mrs. Webster exercised her veto power as his widow and put the kibosh on her late husband's wish.

THE MAN WEBSTER sold his share in the company to was Fred Hall, the stenographer who had risen to partner. By February 1888, Hall had taken charge of the company. He had been in the office long enough to have some sense of what this greater responsibility—and closer connection to the boss—might involve. Back when Hall first took over, Webster hoped his successor would succeed where he had not—and that whenever Hall became thoroughly absorbed in some publishing venture that might rescue the struggling company, Twain wouldn't "want him to drop it or neglect it to revive that 'patent baby clamp' business."

Twain, for his part, was optimistic about their relationship. "You and I," he told Hall, "will never have any trouble."

17

"Get Me Out of Business!"

Twain's vow that he and Hall would never have any trouble was made in all sincerity. Twain trusted the new head of Webster & Company, and their relationship remained strong throughout the six years—from 1888 through 1894—that Hall oversaw the firm's day-to-day operations. These were difficult times. The publishing company's troubles deepened. The debts piled up. But Hall's efforts to make the firm profitable again seem to have touched Twain as those of Webster and other business associates had not. After one unspecified setback, Twain wrote to Hall that Livy

> is deeply distressed, for she thinks I have been blaming you or finding fault with you about something. But most surely that cannot be. I tell [Livy] that although I am prone to write hasty and regrettable things to other people I am not a bit likely to write such things to you. I can't believe I have done anything so ungrateful. If I have, pile coals of fire upon my head, for I deserve it. You

have done magnificently with the business, & we must raise the money [to pay the debts] somehow to enable you to reap a reward for all that labor.

This was the period when events that became known as the Panic of 1893 began to cripple the nation's economy. In June of that year, the stock market crashed, as 500 banks and 16,000 businesses closed their doors. Mines closed, including some of those run by Livy's family; at some that remained open, miners walked off the job. One in four Americans was unemployed, yet Webster & Company continued to operate. Twain praised Hall for managing to "keep the ship afloat in the storm that had seen fleets and fleets go down."

So that Hall could have as much working capital as possible, Twain added, "Mrs. Clemens says I must tell you not to send us any money for a month or two." They would have to get the money—about $500 a month, it seems—from other sources.

These letters to Hall, written in early 1893, were sent from a dilapidated villa outside Florence, Italy. Two years earlier, Twain and Livy had once again come to the conclusion that they could no longer afford to live in Hartford, which had been their home for almost eighteen years. Besides financial worries, Twain was suffering from what medical science in his day called rheumatism. The pain in his right arm, the one he used for writing, was debilitating. This was especially worrisome since he was working on *The American Claimant,* written in haste, for quick money. Twain told Howells he "hoped to sell 100,000 copies of it—no, I mean, 1,000,000." Desperate to keep writing despite the pain in his arm, Twain tried dictating the convoluted farce into an early phonographic recording device. He found this "so awkward for me and so irritating that I not only curse and swear all the time I am dictating, but am impatient and dissatisfied because God has given me only one tongue to curse and swear with." Finally completed in 1891 and published by Webster & Company in 1892, *The American Claimant* had only meager sales.

Livy, who was now forty-seven, had suffered from various illnesses her whole life and, besides rheumatism of her own, was showing signs of heart problems. Livy's physicians recommended the healing waters of Europe's health spas, so Livy and Twain would once more move to Europe. For ready money, Twain secured contracts to write travel articles for American newspapers. They rented out the mansion in Hartford and, on June 6, 1891, sailed for Europe on the *Gascogne,* a steamer "about the same length," Twain said, "as the City of New York." (A big ship was probably a good idea, since the family left New York with twenty-five pieces of luggage.)

Twain told Howells he didn't know how long they would remain in Europe.

> I have a vote but I don't cast it. I'm going to do whatever the others desire, with leave to change their mind, without prejudice, whenever they want to. Travel no longer has any charm for me. I have seen all the foreign countries I want to see except heaven & hell, & I have only a vague curiosity as concerns one of these.

For the next two years, they would more or less wander about the Continent, renting apartments and villas in Italy, Germany, and France. Twain called Aix-en-Provence "the Paradise of the Rheumatics." Germany was "the disease world's bathhouse." They managed to do their share of socializing—Europeans loved Twain's books, and he was recognized wherever they went—but Livy cut household expenses wherever possible. Embarrassed by the increasingly shabby apartments that were all they could afford, they preferred dinners as others' guests to entertaining in their own home as they once had. At one "private feed," as Twain called it, he was seated next to Kaiser Wilhelm II, who "had commanded my presence." The evening did not go well. During dinner, Twain made the unforgiveable faux pas of "making a joyful exclamation of welcome" when the potato was served, without waiting for the kaiser to speak first. Wilhelm II "honestly tried to pretend not to be shocked and outraged, but he plainly was," as were the other six grandees at the table. That was at half past six. The "frost did not get out of the atmosphere" until midnight.

THERE SEEMED A CHILL wherever the family went. Their quarters during these times tended to be dark and drafty, and their spirits sagged. Back when the Paige Compositor was first shown to be able to justify a line of type, Twain had felt a surge of giddy optimism. But that was in early 1889. Four years had come and gone since then, and, to Twain's increasing anger and impatience with Paige, the machine was still being "perfected." It was years from being ready for use by the newspapers, and other firms were already marketing competitive machines. Just before she died in late 1890, Livy's mother had given Twain $10,000 to invest in the machine that he now called "that baby with the Gargantuan appetite."

By the time the family left for Europe in 1891, Twain had invested $74,000 in Webster & Company and $175,000 in the Paige Compositor. Any royalties from Twain's own books went right back into the publishing company, while any other company profits went to bankroll the Paige Compositor. To keep Webster & Company going, Hall had borrowed money from the Mount Morris Bank in Manhattan. The total indebtedness to the bank now came to $30,000. Of that sum, Twain was personally on the hook for $6,000. The bank refused to renegotiate the loans and would soon call them in. Hall was trying to raise additional capital, but, he told Twain, the money market was "beyond description." Twain was still investing $3,000 a month in the company, as well as paying Paige a $7,000 annual salary. Unable to sleep for worrying, Twain would get out of bed at night and pace the floor.*

THE ONLY HOPE now seemed to rest with "that baby with the Gargantuan appetite."

As always, Paige was insistent that all their efforts would soon pay off, but Twain, who persisted in his belief in the machine's commercial possibilities, had begun to lose all faith in the brilliant tinkerer's ability to finish his work. The machine "is superb, it is perfect, it can do 10 men's work. It is worth billions," he told Orion, sounding just like their father when he talked about the Tennessee real estate. And "when the pigheaded lunatic, its inventor, dies, it will instantly be capitalized & make the Clemens children rich."

Paige, however, showed no signs of illness, which Twain struggled mightily to overlook. In May 1892, the inventor reported that he had found a group of investors in Chicago. They were eager not only to invest $3 million in the compositor but would manufacture the machines themselves—fifty in all. With their backing, the Paige Compositor would be demonstrated at

---

* The $74,000 Twain had invested in Webster & Company would come to about $1,830,000 in 2015, the most recent year for which such calculations are available. The investment of $175,000 in the Paige Compositor would be roughly $4 million. Twain's monthly investment of $3,000 in the compositor would be about $74,000 now. Paige's $7,000 annual salary would be approximately $173,000. The publishing company's $30,000 debt to the Mount Morris Bank would be worth some $762,000, with Twain's personal indebtedness of $6,000 worth $168,000.

the World's Columbian Exhibition, which was to open in Chicago in May 1893. The World's Fair, as it came to be known, would be a showcase for all manner of technological innovations: Westinghouse's electrical lighting, Edison's kinetoscope, an electrical kitchen with automatic dishwasher—even the "clasp locker," which eventually became the zipper. The publicity and marketing possibilities were incalculable. Twain, while encouraged, remained somewhat skeptical. Livy was thrilled. "It does not seem credible that we are really going to have money to spend," she told him. "Well I tell you I think I will jump around and spend money just for fun, and give a little away if we really get some."

Eager to see for himself what Paige and the Chicago investors were up to, Twain in late March sailed for America on the *Kaiser Wilhelm*. He spent a few days in New York City, where he had dinner with Andrew Carnegie at the tycoon's home. Carnegie, who ranks second only to John D. Rockefeller on Malcolm Gladwell's list of the richest men in the history of the world (see Chapter 1), was well positioned to be the savior of the Paige Compositor. Twain urged Carnegie to invest in the typesetting machine, reminding the steel magnate of the old adage about not putting all your eggs in one basket. "That's a mistake," Carnegie said. "Put all your eggs in one basket—and watch that basket." This would not be the last time Twain failed to lure Carnegie into one of his schemes, which might be why Carnegie was rich and Twain was not.

Taking Hall with him, Twain spent eleven days in Chicago, much of the time confined to bed with a nasty flu. He hoped to option some of his typesetter royalties to the Chicago investors, but they weren't interested. Paige came to call at Twain's lodgings at the Great Northern Hotel. The meeting was cordial but, it appears, tense. Twain tried to make Paige feel guilty for the interminable delays, and the inventor was "a most daring and majestic liar, absolutely frank in his confessions of misconduct," shedding "even more tears than usual." Then Paige turned the tables on his long-suffering benefactor, saying it "broke his heart" when Twain had left for Europe, leaving "him & the machine to fight along the best way they could."

Apparently, Paige was still negotiating with the Chicago group, which wanted to build a factory to produce the machine, and the negotiations were taking longer than expected—or at least longer than Twain had hoped. They thought they could have a machine finished by July. "The bloody machine offers but a doubtful outlook," Twain told Hall after he had returned to Europe in May. They could expect nothing "for a long time to come; for when the 'three weeks' are up, there will be three months' tinkering to follow, I guess. That is unquestionably the boss machine of the world, but it is the toughest one on prophets . . . that has ever seen the light." All in all, Twain was "disgusted" with the visit.

"Paige and I always meet on effusively affectionate terms," he said. "And yet he knows perfectly well that if I had his nuts in a steel-trap I would shut out all human succor and watch that trap till he died."

Paige evidently believed that big money would soon roll in, or at least he liked to talk as if it would, and not just to Twain, either. On June 10, 1892, under the headline "Sadly Blighted Affections," the *New York Times* reported that a stage actress named Jesse Hall was suing the inventor for breach of promise to marry. She and Paige had moved in together, but he put off the wedding until his invention's earnings would begin to arrive. When that happened, he said he would pay her $800,000. (He was worth between $3 and $4 million, according to the newspapers, though this was clearly untrue.) Paige and his fiancée were content with this arrangement, until he caught his intended "flirting with a good-looking clerk" and abruptly called off the nuptials. The plaintiff's lawyer asked the court to award his client $950,000. How the case was resolved is not known, beyond the obvious fact that the defendant did not have $950,000, and never would. Twain seems not to have known about the lawsuit or said nothing about it if he did. Had he known, it would have provided more fuel for his mounting contempt for Paige.

By August, when Twain returned to the villa in Italy, the situation had not improved. "We are skimming along like paupers, and a day can embarrass us," Twain told Hall. Charles Langdon, Livy's brother, informed her that only about $10,000 of her inheritance remained, and as long as the mines were closed, she could expect no more money from the family business. Livy didn't know how they would get by "unless we sell our house," which they were determined not to do, since they hoped to move back in when conditions improved. The $10,000, she figured, should get them through another year.

Meanwhile, Twain counted up his assets, including his stock in Webster & Company and the copyrights to his books, and thought it came to about $250,000. He doesn't seem to have known what exactly his debts were, but he asked Hall if he thought another publishing company might pay him $200,000 for his debts and for a two-thirds interest in the firm. Twain was still eager to sell his options on the Paige Compositor royalties, but, as should come as no great surprise, no one was interested. What he wanted to hang on to most of all were the royalties on his own books. The fact that he was worried about being able to do so is an indication that he realized he might be forced to sell those as well.

In short, Twain wanted out—out of the publishing business and out of the typesetting business, too, if he could find a way. "I am terribly tired of business," Twain told Hall, being "by nature and disposition unfit for it." He was done with speculation and now wished only to be done with debt. "Get me out of business!"

18

"His Money Is Tainted"

But Hall could not get Twain "out of business," and on August 29, 1893, Twain left Italy and again sailed for New York. There he hoped once more to attend to his messy finances and, if possible, find additional investors for both Webster & Company and the Paige Compositor. Twain arrived on September 7, suffering from a bad cold. For "economy's sake," he checked into the Lotos Club on Fifth Avenue, "drank almost a whole bottle of whisky," and went to bed before dark.

Whiskey enabled him to sleep. Otherwise, Twain continued to pace the floor for hours, trying to figure out just how bad his money problems were and how he might sort them out. The Mount Morris Bank, from which the publishing company and Twain personally had taken loans, was now pressing for immediate repayment of at least $5,000, and Twain had no idea where that money would come from. Even worse, that was only half of the $10,000 that was owed. Livy had budgeted about $5,000 a year for the family to live on, while they carried, by some reckoning, $100,000 in debt. Webster & Company owed them $175,000, and it was failing. Poor Hall, who had stopped drawing a salary, had borrowed $15,000 from family friends.* Twain was terrified that, should the firm go bankrupt, he might lose even the royalties on his past and future books, and "if they go, I am a beggar." Somehow Livy managed to remain hopeful. "Nothing," he said, "daunts [Livy] or makes the world look black to her—which is the reason I haven't drowned myself."

The morning after his first night at the Lotos Club, Twain set off for Hartford, where he hoped to find someone to advance him the $5,000 to pay the bank. Two local businessmen turned him down. Livy once again spoke of selling their Hartford home, which Twain refused to do. He had been willing to consider borrowing against it, but one of the businessmen told him he wouldn't be able to borrow even $3,000 against it, despite the fact that Twain said it was worth $170,000, or $4.5 million in today's dollars. This was a considerable gain over the home's appraisal of $66,650 back in 1877, or maybe just an exaggeration.

Twain also wrote to Susan Crane, Livy's sister by adoption in Elmira, asking if she and her husband could come up with the $5,000, "telling her I had no shame, for the boat was sinking." The Cranes scraped together the money, but any relief Twain might have felt was short-lived. There had been a mistake, Hall informed him. It wasn't $5,000 the bank demanded, but $8,000.

Back in New York City, Twain "raced around Wall Street," he told Livy, "assailing banks and brokers—couldn't get anything." No one was lending money "at any rate of interest whatever or upon any sort of security, or by any*body.*" When he had

---

* The $5,000 owed to the Mount Morris Bank would be about $127,000 in today's dollars. The same is true, obviously, for the money Livy had budgeted for the family's living expenses. The $100,000 debt the Twain family carried would come to roughly $2.5 million in our own time. The $175,000 the publishing company owed the family is worth roughly $4 million. Hall had borrowed, in today's currency, $366,000.

finished his rounds and come up empty-handed, Twain fell onto his bed at eight. Although ruin seemed inevitable, he was "so physically exhausted that mental misery had no chance & I was asleep in a moment."

Within days, Twain was taken in by Clarence Rice, his personal physician, at his home on East 19th Street and Irving Place. Rice was a nose-and-throat specialist to the stars according to Powers, whose A-list patients included Enrico Caruso and Lillian Russell. During their visits, Rice mentioned that he "had ventured to speak to a rich friend of his who was an admirer of mine." Rice had spoken of Twain's financial difficulties to this well-to-do gentleman, and a few evenings later—at Rice's connivance, in all likelihood—Rice and Twain encountered the rich friend in the lobby of the Murray Hill Hotel.

"I want you to know my friend, Mr. H. H. Rogers," Rice said. "He is an admirer of your books."

Twain saw before him a lean, elegantly dressed man with a white mustache, bushy white eyebrows, and an engaging demeanor.

"I was one of your early admirers," Rogers said. "I heard you lecture a long time ago on the Sandwich Islands. I was interested in the subject in those days, and I heard that Mark Twain was a man who had been there. I didn't suppose I'd have any difficulty getting a seat, but I did; the house was jammed. When I came away I realized that Mark Twain was a great man, and I have read everything of yours since that I could get hold of."

When the three men took a seat, Twain told stories. Rogers listened and laughed. As they rose to leave, Rogers suggested that Twain should someday find the time to visit him at his home. He would like Mrs. Rogers to meet him.

Before the three parted, Dr. Rice spoke again.

"Mr. Rogers," he said, "I wish you would look into [Twain's] finances a little. I am afraid they are a good deal confused."

Rogers said he would be happy to do so, and they went their separate ways.

HENRY HUTTLESTON (H. H.) ROGERS entered this world in 1840, during the best possible time in human history to get yourself born, according to Gladwell's *Outliers,* if your intention was to get rich. As a young man in his native Massachusetts, Rogers had clerked in a grocery store, sold newspapers, and served as a baggage master on the railroads. Somehow managing to save $600 by his early twenties, he set off for the newly opened oil fields of Pennsylvania, where he established a small refinery. By 1862, he had gone to work for Charles Pratt & Company, which was based in Brooklyn, where it controlled the distribution of oil throughout the New York City metropolitan area. By 1874, Rogers was working for John D. Rockefeller at the Standard Oil conglomerate, the largest refinery in the world. Rogers rose to vice president and director, overseeing the company's far-flung interests from his office on the eleventh floor of the Standard Oil building at 26 Broadway in Manhattan.

Along the way, Rogers had also developed a reputation as one of the most ruthless tycoons of his day. H. H., critics said, stood for Hell Hound. In 1894, when the conglomerate he and William Rockefeller had formed, the Consolidated Gas Company (later known as Con Ed), became the subject of congressional hearings, Rogers proved "an irascible and contemptuous witness," according to *New York World.* His "share in the unfair and abhorrent methods of Standard Oil was so considerable," the *New York Times* charged, "that he ought therefore to have suffered from increasing torments of remorse, and undoubtedly he did not so suffer." Rogers, the muckraking journalist Ida Tarbell reported, was "as fine a pirate as ever flew his flag on Wall Street." Lewis Leary, the sympathetic editor of the Twain-Rogers correspondence, reports that the tycoon was instrumental in the formation of Amalgamated Copper, the "giant trust built on the corpses of competitors from Boston to Montana, with an initial capital investment of $75,000,000, more than half of which was said to have been in watered stock."

In time, Rogers held corporate positions in copper, gas, steel, electricity, banking, insurance, and railroads. At least he showed no partiality, *New York World* conceded, "grinding up the poor and rich in his money making schemes." The *New York Times* said Rogers "was of that class" that made his great fortune "colossal by not giving the other fellow a fair chance." Commenting on his uncanny ability to escape prosecution for his business methods, the *Wall Street Journal* called him "the Artful Dodger."

At his peak, Rogers would have been worth $40.9 billion in today's money, outranking even his contemporary J. P. Morgan. In the book *The Wealthy 100: From Benjamin Franklin to Bill Gates—A Ranking of the Richest Americans, Past and Present,* Rogers was ranked #22, ahead of Morgan at #23, Bill Gates at #31, and Warren Buffett at #39.

When a friend of Twain's learned that Rogers had taken an interest in his finances, he was appalled. "It's a pity his money is tainted," the friend pointed out.

"It is twice tainted," Twain conceded. "It tain't yours, and it tain't mine."

19

"Mark Twain Loses All"

The day after Twain and Rogers met, Hall set off for the Standard Oil building with the Webster & Company financial books. A series of meetings—often informal, over billiards—followed. Rogers asked questions, and Twain and sometimes Hall explained the situation as best they could. As Rogers saw it, there were two major and interconnected challenges: There was the publishing company, of course, and there was also the matter of the Paige Compositor. Funds from the publishing company's earnings had been used to keep the compositor company operating, as Paige continued to get the machine ready for use. Rogers approached the complexities of the two businesses with calm and reasoned objectivity, which Twain could not do.

Almost instantly, Twain sensed that Rogers's critics might have judged the man too harshly. Although he could be merciless in business, Rogers was also a gregarious fellow, quick-witted and amusing, broad in his interests and enthusiasms, a raconteur with gifts not unlike Twain's own, and another self-made man who enjoyed poker, cigars, billiards, and swearing.

Remarkably loyal and capable of great generosity, Rogers was a friend and benefactor of both Helen Keller and Booker T. Washington.

Before long, Twain had become a regular visitor to his new friend's office, with its commanding view of the Statue of Liberty. Rogers's inner sanctum was a kind of fortress, Twain found, at the entrance to which sat "men who were there by appointment—appointments not loosely specified, but specified by the minute hand of the clock." Twain loved spending time at Rogers's office, "stretched out on a sofa behind his chair, observing his processes," and admiring the unruffled efficiency of his dealings with other captains of industry. Twain was also immensely reassured by the fact that such a capable hand as Rogers would look into his financial troubles and see what, if anything, could be done. Whereas Twain was impulsive and often scatterbrained, Rogers was focused and methodical—"serene, patient, all-enduring," in Twain's words—impressive in the aplomb with which he handled himself.

Twain was also deeply moved by the fact that Rogers was taking any interest at all in another man's troubles. His "time is worth several thousand dollars an hour," but he was not charging his new friend, Mark Twain, a cent. "The only man I care for in the world; the only man I would give a *damn* for; the only man who is lavishing his sweat and blood to save me & mine" he told Livy, was a notorious robber baron.

Over a period of weeks, Rogers came up with a financial plan, both for the publishing company and for the compositor venture. He told Twain to "*stop walking the floor . . .* You may have to go walking again, but don't begin till I tell you my scheme has failed." The scheme involved rescuing both enterprises, while reducing costs and maximizing profits down the road. Twain was hoping Rogers would invest in the Paige Compositor himself, and under the plans Rogers had cooked up, that was a definite possibility. Impressed by the machine, Rogers was keenly aware that whatever technology the newspaper industry adopted, those who held stock in the new technology would make a lot of money. And to that end, Rogers was willing to consider using his own money to bail out both of Twain's financial operations.

Strengthening their own positions—Rogers's as well as Twain's—would require elbowing out all the other investors in the Paige Compositor, the largest being Paige himself. They would need to get rid of him and restructure the company with themselves as sole owners. So, in December 1893, Rogers met with all the investors (except Paige, who was in Chicago) at the Murray Hill Hotel. There he persuaded them that the value of the entire company was not several million dollars, as they supposed, but $276,000. Twain told Livy it was "better than a circus . . . to see Mr. Rogers apply his probe & his bung-starter & remorselessly let the wind & the water" from the company's so-called assets. He let the investors know he was interested in buying their shares in a company that was obviously not worth what they had believed, but that he was also willing to walk if they did not sell at his price. Rogers "sweetly and courteously . . . stripped away all the rubbish," Twain told Livy, and then offered to buy their shares at 20 cents on the dollar. He gave them the rest of the day and night to consider what they might do, but his patience was not unlimited. It was all a bluff —Rogers told Twain he had no intention of walking away— but it worked. Fearing they would lose everything if they didn't accept Rogers's offer, all the investors sold.

Twain and Rogers now controlled all the stock, except for

that portion owned by Paige. They wanted him out of the way, too, except as an employee. Eager "to hang this last remaining scalp on our belt," as Twain said, they took the train to Chicago to meet with the inventor and persuade him to "forsake all previous claims" and accept the terms of the company they were now forming, with themselves as principal stockholders. Meeting with Paige and his lawyer, they told him he was "bankrupt, deep in debt, without credit & without a friend or a well-wisher in the world." Under the circumstances, he should accept their terms. But Paige held out, demanding a payout, a salary, and an assurance that his debts to Pratt & Whitney would be assumed by the new company. Without reaching an agreement, Twain and Rogers took the next train back to New York, knowing, as Rogers told Twain, that Paige "is the only one who *can't* wait." On January 15, 1894, they got word that Paige had agreed to the new terms, giving Twain and his superbly positioned benefactor sole control of the new typesetting technology and its future. Twain was ecstatic.

> I came up to my room and began to undress, and then, suddenly and without warning, the realization burst upon me and overwhelmed me: I and mine, who were paupers an hour ago are rich now and our troubles are over! I walked the floor for half an hour in a storm of excitement. Once or twice I wanted to sit down and cry. You see, the intense strain of three months and a half of daily and nightly work and thought and hope and fear had been suddenly taken away, and the sense of release and delivery and joy knew no way to express itself.

On January 31, Paige came to terms. "Farewell—a long farewell—to *business!*" Twain told Livy. "I will never touch it again! I will live in literature, I will wallow in it, revel in it. I will swim in ink!"

ALL THIS, OF COURSE, was premature—Twain's euphoria, the sense that his money troubles were suddenly behind him, the vow that he was done with business, and the idea that he would forevermore content himself with making a living as a writer. There was still much to be done because Webster & Company continued to hemorrhage money. It was more than $100,000 in debt—about $3 million today—and if the creditors tried to force it into bankruptcy, as seemed likely, they could seize everything Twain owned, including his stock in the new Paige Compositor company.

Here, too, Rogers had a plan, and this one was even more devious than the bluff he sprang on the Paige investors. Initially —and there was nothing remarkable in this—Rogers proposed selling off the eleven-volume *Library of American Literature,* sales of which had screeched to a halt since the Panic of 1893. People just weren't buying expensive sets of literary anthologies —or, apparently, paying for the sets they had ordered. There was about $50,000 in uncollected orders on the Webster & Company ledgers, nearly 600 sets sitting at the warehouse, and another 5,000 sets that had been printed but not yet bound. There were the printer's plates as well. Rogers and a son-in-law who dealt in memorabilia offered $50,000 to buy all of it, on the assumption that, once the depression lifted, sales would rebound. Twain accepted the offer, and Hall threw in some of the office furniture as part of the deal.

This relieved the company of a considerable burden, but there was little reason to believe it could ever become profitable again. Including the Mount Morris Bank, almost a hundred creditors were clamoring for payment, and their demands would have to be met, even if payment was not in full. Few of them could reasonably expect as much, anyway. Managing to keep the Mount Morris Bank at bay, Rogers turned his attention to problems of less immediate urgency but of greater magnitude.

With or without the *Library of American Literature*, Rogers came to realize that the publishing house Charles L. Webster & Company could not be salvaged. Suspecting as much himself, Twain spoke of selling the whole concern. Meanwhile, the Century Publishing Company, which produced *Century* magazine, was interested in buying Twain's company, but only on one condition. Part of the deal would be that the new company would become the sole publisher of Mark Twain's books. Twain considered this unacceptable. But if no other buyer could be found and Webster & Company went under, Twain could lose everything, including his stock in the Paige Compositor and all royalties on all of his books, both those that were already published and those still to come. He had only two sure-fire ways of earning money, and they were connected: writing and lecturing. Twain had grown to hate the lectures, but they were a good way to promote his books and keep his name before the public. They were also lucrative in themselves, but only his writing could be counted on now; he was getting older (he was nearly sixty), his health was declining, and with the passage of years, the rigors of travel took a heavier and heavier toll.

The plan Rogers cooked up would shelter Twain from the financial consequences of Webster & Company's looming collapse. But to accomplish this, Twain must, as soon as possible, transfer all his assets—including his stock in the publishing company and the typesetter company, and the book copyrights and royalties—to his wife. Livy, after all, had lent the firm more than $70,000, which made her its chief creditor. On March 4,

1894, just before he once again sailed back to Europe, Twain signed over power of attorney to Rogers, who prepared the proper documents stating that Twain's assets had been transferred to his wife. Zacks, in *Chasing the Last Laugh,* calls the move "a classic hedge but also a fraudulent transfer. If Webster & Company went under, creditors would find that Twain had no assets."

Then Rogers steered the company into voluntary bankruptcy—filed under New York State law since there was no federal bankruptcy law at this time. Twain's creditors, who, Rogers said, had gleefully planned on "devouring every pound of flesh in sight and picking the bones afterward," were in for a surprise. So were the American people who, picking up their newspapers on April 18, read the front-page headlines. "Failure of Mark Twain," the *New York Tribune* reported. "Mark Twain Fails," cried the *San Francisco Call.* "Mark Twain Loses All," the *New York World* announced. "No Humor Here," the *Washington Times* snickered. The *Brooklyn Eagle* drew a tidy lesson from it all: "It is another case of a shrewd and bright observer of things missing a moral which he could readily have taught to other people."

Though embarrassed by all the unfavorable publicity, Twain told reporters he was "relieved" by the bankruptcy. This, friends reminded him, was standard business procedure. Livy, back in Europe, was ashamed and saw it all as a moral failure. Twain tried to reassure her there was nothing dishonorable in what he had done and that, in time, their debts would be paid and their creditors made whole. This belief that no one would be stiffed was kept alive, no doubt, because Twain still hoped that in the coming months the Paige Compositor would pay off royally. Livy had wanted to sign over the Hartford house to the other creditors, worried that the preference given to her by the transfer of assets was unfair to them. Twain had taken that action, he told her, because his chief duty was to her and the children, "my second is to those others. I must protect you first," even if it meant protecting her from the consequences of her own admirable generosity and sense of fair play.

Twain told Livy that at meetings with the creditors, he struggled to remember how Rogers had instructed him to speak of the family's assets.

"It was confoundedly difficult at first for me to be always saying, 'Mrs. Clemens's books,' 'Mrs. Clemens's copyrights,' 'Mrs. Clemens's type-setter stock,' & so on, but it was necessary to do this, & I got the hang of it presently. I was even able to say with gravity, 'My wife has two unfinished books, but I am not able to say when they will be completed or where she will elect to publish them when they are done.'"

In August of 1894, with the details of the settlement still to be decided, Twain left to join his family in Europe. In October the Paige Compositor and other typesetting machines, including Mergenthaler's, were to be pitted against one another at trials by the *Chicago Herald*.

Now all Twain had to do was wait for the competition and, once the newspapers had learned the results, watch the money roll in.

20

"Knocked Flat on My Back"

The *Chicago Herald*'s sixty-day trial of the Paige Compositor began on September 20, 1894. Back in Paris, Twain eagerly awaited updates. At first, the machine seemed to be performing so magnificently that the Mergenthaler backers "will come and want to hitch teams with us." Rogers soon reported, however, that the trial was not going as well as hoped after all. Their machine, while undoubtedly speedy, was also error-prone. Also, type tended to break. Paige had to be summoned personally for repairs because the machine proved so complex that no one but its inventor understood how, once there was a glitch, to get it operating properly again. It was too delicate, the *Herald* owners were coming to realize, for them to rely on. Twain stuck by the machine. When it is "in proper working order," he insisted, "it cannot make a mistake." The problem must be the operator, he told Rogers, and urged him not to take this mere hiccup seriously.

Again Twain waited, and as he did, his health declined. He "got knocked flat on my back with gout," which he first assumed was "some new kind of super-devilish rheumatism, and imagined it would stop hurting presently. But it didn't," he told Rogers. Twain was able to sleep from midnight to 3 a.m., which was followed by "5 or 6 hours wherein the gout was the only presence present." Gout is "one of the oldest pains known to medical science, and is perhaps the most competent. When we got the doctor at last, he said it was only the gout, and an attack of no importance. He seemed to regard it as a pleasure trip. He gave me a hypodermic and appeared to think the business was done—which it wasn't." Another injection helped, but Twain was in pain again the next day. As for the doctor's opinion that the gout was of no consequence, Twain told Rogers, Hell is of no consequence, either, "to a person who doesn't live there."

By late November, Twain's health was better but reports on the Paige Compositor only got worse. The machine still was not performing as hoped, which made Twain doubt the whole enterprise and its future—and himself. Maybe they had added too many unnecessary features to the machine (did it really need a key that made the sign for pi?). Maybe they had rushed the whole process. But "that would have been *fore*sight, whereas hindsight is my specialty . . . My hindsight," he realized, "is getting to be very sharp." It grieved Twain that, although Rogers had "put so much money and brains, and good hard work into that machine there was nobody to save you from this disappointment. I am to blame." Rogers would come out of all this fine, Twain realized, but he himself would not. When he heard from Chicago, he braced himself. He would shiver and tell himself to "stand by for a cyclone! for if Mr. Rogers finds it wise and best to remove his supports from under that machine, your fine ten-year-old dream will blow away like a mist and you will land in the poor house sure."

Hope in the Paige Compositor was not dead, but it was dying. If the trials failed completely (as seemed increasingly likely), and Rogers pulled out, they should consider making no announcement of Rogers's decision to withdraw his backing. This delay would give them time to buy Mergenthaler stock "at as low a figure as possible." Surely the Mergenthaler stock would then boom, "for their machine will then be the cock of the walk, and *permanently,* without possibility of rivalry." With the Paige invention out of the way, the Mergenthaler would be "an absolutely sure investment."

Twain tried to work—he was finishing up the solemn *Personal Recollections of Joan of Arc,* one of his least successful novels—and to face facts. His fifty-ninth birthday had come and gone. Livy and their children "spent two francs on birthday presents for me, and we have begun life on a new and not altogether unpromising basis."

A FEW DAYS before Christmas, Twain received the news he was dreading: The Paige Compositor, Rogers decided, was a bust. He and his money were out of the deal. Deprived of Rogers's future investment, the company would have to be dissolved.

As inevitable as it might have been, the news of Rogers's decision nevertheless "knocked every rag of sense out of my head," Twain said, "and I went flying here and there and yonder, not knowing what I was doing, and only one clearly defined thought standing up visible and substantial out of the crazy storm-drift —that my dream of ten years was in desperate peril, and out of the 60,000 or 70,000 projects for its rescue that came flocking through my skull, not one would hold still long enough for me to examine it and size it up."

Desperate, Twain decided he could scurry back to Chicago,

or New York, or Hartford—wherever—and see for himself if the venture might be rescued. "I must be there and see it die. That is, if it must die; and maybe if I were there we might hatch up some next-to-impossible way to make it take up its bed and take a walk." For four hours, such fantasies tormented him and, "still whirling," he even checked the schedules for trains and ships, "with just barely head enough left on my shoulders to protect me from being used as a convenience by the dogs." By bedtime, Livy "had reasoned me into a fairly rational and contented state of mind; but of course it didn't last long." Then he dashed off lists of possible alterations to the machine, in hopes of accomplishing what Paige had spent years trying to do: perfect the unwieldy contraption, including dispensing with half the keyboard, with its "diphthongs, fractions, & other rubbish which heavily load us up with machinery and yet are used but very very seldom." But an argument based on such small details would not persuade an expansive strategic mind like Rogers's, and it didn't.

Rogers, by contrast, took the long view. The Paige Compositor "was a marvelous invention," he admitted, and his assessment suggests a sense that a machine of its kind would be practical only in a future day, when machines might be more like people, perhaps in the Artificial Intelligence sense. The machine, Rogers said, "was the earliest approach to a human being in the wonderful things it could [do] of any machine I had ever known. But that was just the trouble; it was too much of a human being and not enough of a machine. It has all the complications of the human mechanism, all the liability of getting out of repair, and it could not be replaced with the ease and immediateness of the human being. It was too costly; too difficult of construction; too hard to set up."

• • •

STILL REELING OVER THE NEWS, Twain also considered alterations to his family's lives that might relieve them of some of their burdens. He realized they could never again afford to live in the Hartford house—"though it would break the family's hearts"—and would need to find more or less permanent tenants. It was costing them $200 a month just to hold on to the mansion. That's $5,400 today. "If we can rent, or sell, or burn the house," it would save a lot of money.

"The thing for me to do," he told Rogers shortly after New Year's, "is to teach myself to endure a way of life which I was familiar with during the first half of my life but whose sordidness and hatefulness and humiliation long ago faded out of my memory and feeling." This is a remarkable admission, coming so late in life. Twain never spoke of his early years as ones of suffering and deprivation, but it seems that is how the author of the idyllic *Tom Sawyer* might really have recalled them. "With the help of my wife this will not be very difficult, I think. I think, indeed, that she and I could adjust ourselves to the new conditions quite easily if we were alone,—in fact, I know it—but the reflection that they are going to be hard on the children" would make the adjustment more difficult.

He then wrote to notify friends in Hartford that the house was for rent. Livy's family business seemed to have revived somewhat from the Panic of 1893, and they could live on about $4,000 a year—just over $100,000 today—from the Langdon interests in Elmira. Twain figured he could count on another $3,500 from the books that were still in print. "To that," he told Rogers, "I must add $5,000 a year by work, and that will keep the tribe alive." They weren't sure where they would live but were thinking of going home. The difficulty of living in New York was that Livy was not strong enough to walk the distances between the horse-car lines. But neither of them wanted "to live elsewhere in America—certainly not in Hartford, in the circumstances." They would definitely return in the spring, and he would spend the summer in Elmira writing and revising, with *Joan of Arc* slated for release by the end of the year.

At least in New York Twain would be among friends, with whom he would have no reason for embarrassment. He would also be near Rogers, to whom he felt indebted—morally and personally, though not financially. Rogers was afraid that his decision to pull out of the Paige investment would cost him his friendship with Twain. But he need not have worried. Twain said he'd never had a better friend in his life. He would soon turn sixty, and in all those years, he said, "I never had a friend before who put out a hand and tried to pull me ashore when he found me in deep waters."

Rogers had involved himself with patience and great skill, and if he had not made all Twain's troubles go away, he had banished a great deal of them. Even if they had settled nothing, their meetings in Rogers's Wall Street office had been a great blessing. He had seen the man dealing with far graver matters than his own miserable affairs, and Rogers was a model of grace and good humor.

> Every day those consultations supplied . . . plenty of vexations and exasperations for Mr. Rogers—I know this quite well—but if ever they found revealment in his face or manner it could have been for only a moment or two, for the signs were gone when he re-entered his private office, and he was always his brisk and cheerful self again and ready to be chaffed and joked, and reply in kind. His spirit was often heavily burdened, necessarily, but it cast no shadow, and those about him always sat in the sunshine.

In coming years, Twain and Rogers would spend days and weeks together, sometimes in Rogers's private train car, or on his yacht. Twain's writer friends didn't understand or accept his fondness for Rogers, but Twain never apologized for it. Once, when Twain suggested Rogers as a guest at one of their luncheons, Finley Peter Dunne, author of the Mr. Dooley newspaper pieces, questioned the choice.

"I thought you said this was to be a literary lunch."

"So it is," Twain said.

"Then why ask Rogers?"

"Why ask Rogers? Why ask Rogers? To pay for the lunch, you idiot."

WITHIN WEEKS of the compositor's collapse, Twain was feeling hopeful again and full of schemes. Rogers shouldn't worry, Twain said, because he had come up with a plan to escape the "heavy nervous strain" that Twain and Livy had been living with for months now—"another project" that would enable them to pay their debts. Rogers should "take a breath and stand by for a surge."

Details of this grand plan would follow soon.

21

"Money for a Monument"

The grand plan was for Twain to embark on a world tour, lecturing to paying crowds for a year, with stops in Australia, New Zealand, India, and South Africa. Twain would take Livy and their daughter Clara with him. He wanted Rogers and his wife and son to accompany them, but Rogers demurred. He would stay home in New York, receiving the checks that Livy would forward to him. Livy, who figured it would take four years to free themselves from their "bondage of debt," would do all the bookkeeping, filling pages with "acres of figures." She would send the earnings, less the agent's percentage, back to Rogers. These he would use for the reimbursement of Webster & Company creditors. Whatever was left, he would save for them or look to invest.

Going back on the lecture circuit was something Twain dreaded. He had declared before that he would never again mount the platform and play the fool for the amusement of strangers. He hated pretending to enjoy the dinners he was obliged to attend when he spoke around the country—the nineteenth-century's rubber-chicken circuit—and he found traveling from town to town in drafty railcars and staying in small-town hotels increasingly wearisome. "I guess I am out of the field permanently," he had declared shortly after he had gotten married. "Have got a lovely wife; a lovely house, bewitchingly furnished; a lovely carriage and a coachman whose style and dignity are simply awe-inspiring—nothing less—and I am making more money than necessary—by considerable, and therefore why crucify myself nightly on the platform?"

But that seemed a long time ago. Twain no longer had the energy that he was blessed with as a younger man, and now felt no need to advertise himself as he had done when he was nobody. Now he was so famous it seemed his every embarrassment made the papers. Still, he saw no alternative, since he was good at lecturing, there was always a demand for his appearances, and there was ready money in it. His agent had recommended a lecture tour as soon as he had learned of Twain's bankruptcy. "I hope your business troubles will not break you down," the agent wrote. "It comes hard at this stage of the game but with your vigor of mind and body I cannot imagine a better equipped veteran for a hard fight." And a hard fight it would be. He had done plenty of lecturing in America. "This time," as Resa Willis writes in *Mark and Livy,* "the world would be his stage."

THEY LEFT ELMIRA by rail on July 14, 1895. Twain made an appearance in Cleveland, then "lectured and robbed and raided" his way to Vancouver, British Columbia, playing twenty-two cities in thirty-eight days. Twain told his admirers he was confident that if he lived through the ordeal he could pay off the debt, "after which, at the age of sixty-four, I can make a fresh and unincumbered [*sic*] start in life."

They covered 2,500 miles in railcars—and did fifteen appearances—before sailing to Australia on August 23. By mid-September Twain was doing two weeks of lecturing in Australia, and from there to New Zealand before returning to Australia a week or so before Christmas.

He was a huge hit among the Aussies. For every appearance, at least a thousand people showed up. It was "constant unceasing adulation of Papa," Clara recalled. Shortly after New Year's they were off to Ceylon, where the demand was so great that he had to give three lectures a day. Next came India, from January 20 to April 1, followed by almost two months of much-needed rest and relaxation in Mauritius. But Twain was painfully aware of the need to press on. Whenever he was ill and couldn't speak, Livy figured they lost $500 a day. So Twain soldiered on, despite colds and carbuncles. "I am sure if his life & health are spared to him that it will not be long until he is out of debt," Livy wrote to her sister. "Won't that be one joyful day."

Things really were looking up. Twain wrote travel pieces for the *Century* magazine, much as he had done for newspapers in his *Innocents Abroad* days decades earlier. He would turn those articles into a book, *Following the Equator,* for the American Publishing Company. The $10,000 advance—$270,000 today —went directly to Rogers for safekeeping. So did profits from the lectures. There were also earnings from *The Tragedy of Puddin'head Wilson,* serialized in the *Century* magazine and then released in hardcover in late 1894, with unanticipated profits from a stage version that opened in March 1895. The same year *Puddin'head Wilson* was published, *Tom Sawyer Abroad* hit the bookstores, followed by *Tom Sawyer, Detective* two years later. *Joan of Arc* was also published in 1896. *Following the Equator* came out the next year.

"What had started for him as a desperate lunge for money," Zacks writes in *Chasing the Last Laugh,* "was starting to seem magically transformed into a victory lap for the 'humorist of the century.'" The thousands of people who had read about Twain's financial difficulties in the newspapers were also now following his heroic efforts to claw his way back. Upon receipt of payment, creditors were writing thank-you notes that Rogers saved and passed along to Twain and Livy. "I appreciate [Twain's] manliness no less than his incomparable humor," wrote one sales agent who had finally gotten the $3.27 coming to him. "For the first time in my life," Twain told Rogers, "I am getting more pleasure out of paying money out than pulling it in." To William Dean Howells he wrote, "I hope you will never get the like of the load saddled onto you that was saddled onto me three years ago. And yet, there is such a solid pleasure in *paying* the things that I reckon maybe it is worth while [*sic*] to get into that kind of hobble."

WITH THE TOUR finally completed, the family sailed in July 1896 for Southampton, England. There they lived while Twain worked on *Following the Equator* and rested. But in August, family tragedy struck. While visiting Hartford, their twenty-four-year-old daughter Susy, who had chosen not to accompany Clara and their parents on the world tour, was diagnosed with spinal meningitis. While Livy and Clara sailed home to nurse her, a telegram informed Twain, back in England, that Susy had died.

For several months, Susy's grief-stricken father became something of a recluse. Despite the upturn in the family's finances, Twain's uncharacteristic absence from social events gave rise to heartless rumors. People said he had been abandoned by his family and was penniless. In response to these rumors, the *New York Herald* began a charity drive to bail him out and put in $1,000 of seed money. Andrew Carnegie pledged another $1,000, and the paper asked for donations. Contributions of as little as 5 cents were welcome.

When Livy found out about the charity drive, she was mortified. Rogers, troubled too, wired Twain, urging him to "retire gracefully." Adding to the overall embarrassed discombobulation, Twain admitted that he was aware of the newspaper's efforts on his behalf and, in fact, had approved the scheme back when "everything was looking black and hopeless." There is even some evidence that he *initiated* the idea, although he claimed to have forgotten the details. Had he ever broached the subject with Livy, he said, "she would have forbidden me to touch it—and for that reason I didn't mention it to her." What concerned him most, he told Rogers, was that the charity drive "may end in a humiliating failure and show me that I am not very popular."

His rationale, in what appears to have been a letter intended for the *Herald,* makes a kind of loopy sense:

> This way out (of debt) would not have occurred to me, and a year or two ago my self-love would have rebelled; but I have grown so tired of being in debt that often I think I would part with my skin and my teeth to get out. I know that the custom is to wait till a man is dead and then gather up money for the monument for him when he can't enjoy it; but if friends want to collect advance money for a monument now, my creditors will think that the wiser more rational course, and so shall I. If I can get on my feet again I will be the monument myself, and shan't even need another one.

The effort did in fact prove to be the "humiliating failure" that Twain feared. Hoping to jump-start the fund drive, Twain suggested a scheme that, as might be expected, involved Rogers and his deep pockets. "I wish you would collect $40,000 privately for me from yourself," he wrote, "then pay it back to yourself, and have somebody tell the press it was collected but by [Livy's] desire (and mine) I asked that it be returned to the givers and that it was done . . . Now if your conscience will let you do that, it will reverse things and give me a handsome boom, and nobody will ever be the wiser. I like the idea. I don't see any harm in it." But Livy, who disapproved of every aspect of the scheme, *did* see harm in it. Twain told the *Herald* to cease the drive and return the money, which it did, putting a finis to the entire fiasco.

THE FAMILY MOVED around Europe before returning home to America. They spent two years in Vienna. There Twain's popularity was such that their apartment became what Resa Willis calls "a second American embassy," with Twain, as he put it, functioning as "self-appointed ambassador-at-large of the United States of America — without salary." Livy got "millions of delight" during these years, methodically tracking the reduction in their debts, which she figured could be zero by January 1898. And she was right. At the end of the month, Rogers informed them that they were in the clear, and with $12,000 to $13,000 left over. Using some of these funds and more that came in later, Rogers began making savvy investments for Twain, more than doubling their nest egg.

Virtually all biographers who have written about Twain's financial problems report that he paid his debts in full. But this really wasn't the case, as Zacks points out in *Chasing the Last Laugh*. The biographers also routinely claim that Twain had been legally obligated to pay only 50 cents on the dollar but, as a man of honor, had voluntarily paid back every penny. Here too Zacks sets the record straight. This conventional account, he notes, omits inconvenient realities. In fact, three major creditors, including the Mount Morris Bank, had sued and won judgments against him, totaling more than $30,000. It was not Twain but Livy who insisted they pay in full even when creditors agreed in separate negotiations to accept less than 100 percent. Moreover, Zacks writes, Twain never did pay the Mount Morris Bank. Biographers have also failed to examine the shift of assets from Twain to Livy just prior to the bankruptcy, which Zacks calls fraudulent.

Twain, while not a good businessman, was a superb manager of his own image—an image he created, publicized, and, when damaged, contrived to rehabilitate. He put his own spin on his money problems so successfully that the public, which had looked askance at his excesses and extravagances, just as quickly celebrated him as a selfless soul who had struggled against financial setbacks and triumphed as few could. When, on October 15, 1900, the *Minnehaha* brought Twain, Livy, and Clara back to New York City, reporters were waiting on the dock, eager to welcome the returning hero.

Two days before the ship came into port, the *New York Times* set the tone for his reception. Having "long lived down the invidious reputation of a mere maker of jokes," the *Times* said, Twain on both sides of the Atlantic has established himself "as one of the first of living writers of the English language." But it is not mainly as a man of letters that Twain's countrymen have reason to be proud of him.

> It is as an American who has shown that the American standard of honor goes far beyond the standard set by the law. Many acts of commercial honor have been done by Americans which showed as high and scrupulous a

sense of what was due from man to man as the assumption by [Twain] of debts for which he was not legally liable. But the conspicuousness of the position of a popular author makes his example in such a matter more useful for edification of his own countrymen, and far more valuable to them as a vindication of the National character abroad. No foreigner will be apt to repeat without shame the old sneers at "Yankee sharp practice" who remembers this signal exhibition of "that sensibility of principle, that chastity of honor, which feels a stain like a wound."

22

"You Cannot Lose a Penny"

When William Dean Howells first laid eyes on Twain and Livy, he said they looked ten years younger than they had before they left on their world tour. He was sixty-four and she was fifty-four, but they seemed to radiate a "renewed youth." Livy saw it, too, in her husband. He now behaved like a "fighting cock," she said.

None of this surprised Twain. Their good health was attributable, he said, to a diet, the basis of which was a powdered food supplement derived from waste products fed to pigs. He had discovered it when they lived in Vienna two years ago. It was known as Plasmon and had developed a following on the Continent. The German manufacturers said three pounds of Plasmon was nutritionally equivalent to 100 pints of milk. The family had come to rely on Plasmon, he told Rogers. "Among us we can eat about a quarter of a pound of it per day," which Twain claimed supplied the same nourishment as four pounds of steak. A pound of Plasmon "contains the nutriment of 16 lbs. of beef, and will do the same nourishing that the 16 lbs. would do, besides being no trouble to digest." It is "pure albumin," with "neither taste nor smell." It dissolves readily, and, Twain added with scientific precision, "99.4 percent of it digests."

Twain had tried it and then encouraged Livy to try it, too, since her health, which was never good, continued to decline. Nothing else had seemed to help. She was barely able to keep solid food down when they lived in Austria. She had tried to eat an egg once, washed down with a half teaspoonful of malted milk, but the combination "acted like poisons—numbed her arms and distributed pains over a large nerve-surface." She detested Plasmon, Twain admitted, "yet she has to live on it, as far as keeping up her strength goes." Twain had three doctors attending to his wife, and he "implored them all to feed the madam solely on Plasmon for three days," but after trying the regimen, "they got scared and went to guessing again and raised some more hell."

At last, "having tried everything else and failed," one of the physicians consented to a twenty-four-hour trial, and the results were "so good that the madam is herself almost convinced, and is willing to chance another 24. The only strength she had got [is] from the Plasmon that was mixed with the failures—as the doctor has to admit." Livy, however, was less enthusiastic. When she learned he was urging Rogers to adopt the regimen, she was "greatly troubled about that Plasmon cure," Twain admitted. She instructed him to tell Rogers "to *boil* it before using it." Evidently, it did not go down as smoothly as Twain said. Whether Plasmon helped or harmed Livy is impossible to know at this late date. But it is clear that she hated the stuff—and evidently did not want Rogers to suffer as she had.

Twain tried to get Howells to make Plasmon part of his routine, too. "Yes—take it as medicine—there is nothing better, nothing surer of desired results," Twain said. "If you wish to be elaborate—which isn't necessary—put a couple of heaping teaspoonfuls of the powder in an inch of milk & stir it until it is a paste; put it in some more milk and stir the paste to a thin gruel; then fill up the glass and drink. Or, stir it into your soup. Or, into your oatmeal. Or, use it any method you like, so's you *get it down*—that is the only essential."

It never failed to astonish Twain that otherwise sensible people—especially medical doctors—could be so irrationally resistant to such wonderful breakthroughs in modern medicine. "The scientific testimonials," he told Rogers, "are strong enough to float Gibraltar." It seemed obvious to Twain that Plasmon, in Resa Willis's paraphrase, could "feed the world's hungry and cure the world's sick." It also seemed obvious to Twain—and this could not have come as too great a surprise to Rogers—that Plasmon would be a sure-fire investment, making untold millions for anyone who got in on the ground floor.

Twain had been itching to invest again almost as soon as he was back on his feet. It didn't take long for him to find his next sure thing—and Plasmon was not the first item that captured his interest. In mid-March 1898, he learned of a young Austrian, Jan Szczepanik, who claimed to have invented a machine to revolutionize the Jacquard loom, which used punch cards to make complex patterns on the carpets it wove. Szczepanik's invention, as Twain described it, "automatically punches the holes in the Jacquard cards, and does it with mathematical accuracy" —and at a third of the cost of methods already in use.

Dazzled by the possibilities, Twain turned himself into an instant expert on carpet weaving by poring over the best carpeting statistics he could find at the U.S. embassy in Vienna. These statistics were eighteen years old and, he realized, of limited value. Even so, he met the next day with Szczepanik and his banker, who were "merely expecting to find a humorist, not a commercial cyclopedia." Twain peppered them both with questions, and the money man said Twain "could get my living as a financier if authorship should fail me." Twain wanted in, and negotiations ensued. "I've landed a big fish to-day," he told Rogers. For an unspecified sum, he agreed to take an option to buy the North American rights for $1.5 million. Of course, he needed additional investors, which is where Rogers came in. They could corner the carpet-weaving market and establish a monopoly, which other plutocrats were busily trying to establish in their respective industries. In fact, Standard Oil should consider buying it all, "and take the fish off my hands, and give me one-tenth of that Company's stock, fully paid up, for my share." Standard Oil could make 200 percent a year from its investment.

> Competition would be at an end in the Jacquard business, on this planet. Price-cutting would end. Fluctuations in values would cease. The business would be the safest and surest in the world; commercial panics could not seriously affect it; its stock would be as choice an investment as Government bonds. When the patents died the Company would be so powerful that it could still keep the whole business in its hands and strangle competition. Would you like to grant me the privilege of placing the whole Jacquard business of the world in the grip of a single Company? And don't you think the business would *grow*—grow like a weed?

Twain was convinced that this investment was sound; this time around would be different. As evidence, Twain passed along a pamphlet on this new process to Rogers so he could see for himself. Carpets could spill out of the looms almost immediately, Twain told Rogers. This time the company "will not have to wait, and wait, and wait, and chew its bowels, and moan about hope deferred, and all that. (Because it isn't a type-setter.)"

With characteristic good sense, Rogers consulted an expert of his own choosing to look into the business — someone who actually worked in the textile field and knew something about it. "I do not feel that it would be of any value to us in our mills, and the number of Jacquard looms in America is so limited that I am of the opinion that there is no field for a company to develop the invention here," the expert reported. "A cursory examination of the pamphlet leads me to place no very high value upon the invention, from a practical standpoint."

At that, Twain dropped the idea, though doing so was difficult, for Szczepanik's money man had other brilliant ideas. (One was a method for making blankets out of peat moss, when mixed with cotton, "or with wool if you want better goods." They claimed that using this process they could make a suit of clothes — "soft, good, and durable" — for 36 cents.)

IN MARCH 1900, Twain again decided that it "was about time for me to look around and buy something," he told Rogers. "So I looked around and bought." The company in Germany that produced Plasmon was forming a British affiliate to market it there, which presented a once-in-a-lifetime opportunity. Seizing it, Twain invested $12,500 (and at least that much later on) and was made the new company's president, which prompted a move to London to oversee operations. By 1901, the British firm was shipping up to eight tons of Plasmon per month, and Twain was earning more than $1,500 in quarterly dividends. "It's as good as railroading," he told Rogers. He could easily "clear 20,000 [pounds sterling] a month." Maybe so, but Rogers remained skeptical. "I'm afraid you think Plasmon is a speculative thing, but really it isn't," Twain insisted. "I'm not running any risk . . . You cannot lose a penny."

But so what if Rogers didn't want to invest in Plasmon? Others surely would. Andrew Carnegie, maybe. Hoping to get Carnegie on board, Twain adopted the well-intentioned but questionable tactic of writing not to Carnegie himself, but to the tycoon's daughter, Margaret, then three years old. He suggested that Margaret—or whoever read the letter—give her father "five or six fingers of Scotch," and then talk to him about Plasmon. "This will mellow him up and enlarge his views, and before he solidifies again you will have him. That is to say, you will have his cheque for £500 drawn to order of 'Plasmon Syndicate, Ltd.' which you will send to me, and you and I will be personally responsible that the money is back in his hands in six months, and along with it 500 shares in the Plasmon Company, all paid up." Even if charmed by this novel approach, Carnegie did not invest.

This was no doubt wise. In 1900 Twain came back to the United States to form the American Plasmon Company, investing $25,000 of his own money to do so and acting as its president. The new company was incorporated in 1902, but within two years, Twain admitted to Rogers that it was "one of those investments of mine that I am ashamed of, and would like to forget." For reasons he didn't specify, he apparently had never been able to pay close enough attention to its operations, and the company suffered as a result—though not as much, maybe, as it would have had he paid close attention. He even considered making additional investments in it, though he suspected Rogers "would consider an additional purchase an additional insanity. That is what it would have been, I think."

In late 1907, with Twain as its president, the American Plasmon Company was sued by three former officers. Twain admitted that the company, with only $13.08 in its bank account, was unable to pay its bills and was now bankrupt. When the company's receivers obtained a court order to get its account books, the *New York Times* reported, "Mark Twain is at present in Bermuda." (He was vacationing, though the *Times* did not say so.)

When reporters finally reached Twain, they asked if it was true, as rumored, that he felt he had been swindled.

"It is," he told them.

"Out of how much?"

"Oh, about $32,000. I held $25,000 worth of the stock, and one of the members of the company swindled me out of the $12,500 later. No, I won't say I was swindled out of the $25,000. The company failed because of bad management. I ought not to say I was swindled out of all the money. Most of it was lost through bad business. I was always bad in business."

But maybe that was too harsh a judgment. "If I had kept out of American Plasmon," he told Rogers, "I would now be a good business man, but as it is, I am only half a good business man."

In late 1909, just six months before Twain's death, the Plasmon venture ended, taking Twain's entire investment with it. But this failure did little to squash this irrepressible man's high spirits: When Twain crowed next about an opportunity to invest $50,000 in a new railroad that Rogers hadn't heard of and that didn't seem to be included in standard railroad industry listings, Rogers told him, "Do be careful. It is much easier to keep out of trouble than it is to get out. You and I know that of old."

23

"To Succeed in Business . . ."

It was in 1897, when Twain was living in London, that rumors that he had suddenly died began to spread back in the United States. In early summer, the *Cincinnati Inquirer* reported that "broken down, mentally and physically, his once brilliant mind incapable of further effort and almost penniless, his life is drawing to a close." Other papers picked up the doleful tone, which led to the publication of obituaries. The *New York Herald* tried to sum up Twain's life, drawing some platitudinous lessons about why he had lost so much money. "Had he been less of a humorist," the *Herald* speculated, "he might have been more of a business man."

On June 2, a cub reporter for the *New York Journal* showed up at the house Twain had rented in London. When Twain refused to get out of bed to meet him, the reporter sent up the telegram he had been given, which reminds us once again of the many ways a man can be worth more dead than alive. "If Mark Twain dying in poverty, in London, send 500 words," the telegram read. "If Mark Twain has died in poverty, send 1000 words."

Twain sent back a handwritten note, explaining that he had a cousin in London who had been seriously ill a few weeks earlier but had since recovered. "The report of my illness grew out of his illness," Twain wrote. "The report of my death was an exaggeration." (Evidently, he never actually said reports of his death were "greatly exaggerated.") "Of course I am dying," he told the *Journal's* London bureau chief, "but I'm not dying faster than anybody else." The notion that he was impoverished, however, he found "harder to deal with" than reports that he had died. The *Journal* duly corrected the record, telling its readers that Twain was living comfortably in a splendid house in Chelsea.

Twain, who was sixty-one in 1896, still had another fourteen years ahead of him. These were difficult years, marked — as are the last years of most people who live long lives — by failing health and the deaths of loved ones. After their world tour, Twain and Livy had moved around a good deal, usually in the vain hope that she would flourish in a different climate, under a different regimen or with more mineral baths, and would eventually regain strength. After their return to New York, they rented a house in Riverdale, on the Hudson River, in 1901 but left two years later for Italy. There on June 5, 1904, in a villa overlooking Florence, Livy died at the age of fifty-eight, having suffered for years from heart and thyroid problems.

After her funeral and burial in Elmira, Twain lived at 21 Fifth Avenue in New York City. In 1908, he moved to a house he had built and named Stormfield in Redding, Connecticut, about sixty-five miles northeast of New York City. It was at Stormfield on Christmas Eve, 1909, that his daughter Jean Clemens, who was an epileptic, died of a heart attack suffered during a seizure.

She was twenty-nine. (Twain's only surviving daughter, Clara Clemens Samossoud, the only one to marry and produce a grandchild, lived to be eighty-eight years of age. She died in November 1962 in La Jolla, California.) Bedeviled by bronchitis and angina, brought low by grief, Twain died of heart failure at Stormfield on April 21, 1910. Seventy-five at the time of death, he was buried in Elmira, next to Livy.

There were times of great loneliness during Twain's last years, but he never again had to worry about money—even if he was in the habit of doing so. Once Rogers got him out of financial trouble, Twain prospered, despite his best efforts to lose it all on the carpet-weaving business, on Plasmon, and on a succession of less noteworthy schemes. Rogers invested in blue-chip stocks for him, and having enabled Twain to hold on to the copyrights for his own books, Twain continued to profit from their sale in various editions. Stage productions of his books also brought in revenue. Twain's world tour increased his popularity and book sales in other countries that already knew and loved his books. The American Publishing Company issued the first collected volume of all of his works in the late 1890s.

BY THE TIME of Twain's death, he was arguably the most famous American in the world and easily the most photographed. There's film footage of him available online, supposedly taken by Thomas Edison. In it Twain can be seen walking outside Stormfield in 1909, using a slightly comical shambling gait, with white hair, white suit, cigar, and all. Twain's was an instantly recognizable image in his own day. The pseudonym he had adopted in his newspaper days as well as his likeness were used to advertise and sell all sorts of products, and pretty much all without obtaining his permission and without paying him. There were Mark Twain brands of whiskey, cigars, tobacco, playing cards, ashtrays, fans, flour, board games, calendars, train cars, shaving soap, sewing machines, china, and—a little later—Oldsmobiles. There was, by one account, a jumping frog mechanical bank. The card game Authors included Twain (before his hair turned white) in 1873. Sheet music distributed in 1911 for "There Isn't Anyone for Me to Play With Anymore" had his picture on the cover.

There were Mark Twain shirts and trousers, shoes, socks and underwear, and, for the ladies, Mark Twain mink coats. Twain would have approved, provided, of course, he was properly compensated. He believed in wearing clothes. "Clothes make the man," he is supposed to have said, though the quote might be apocryphal. "Naked people have very little influence in society."

OBSERVING ALL THIS, marketing geniuses today still draw supposedly profound lessons about their own profession from how the man we know as Mark Twain managed his extraordinary career and, as we would say today, his "personal brand." Marketing consultants say Twain was a global brand, and that was no doubt true, as the success of his lectures in other countries amply demonstrated. We can learn a great deal about "content marketing" from Twain, Owen Matson tells us on MarketScale.com. In his book *What Mark Twain Learned Me 'bout Public Speakin'*, motivational speaker Conor Cunneen says we can make better presentations by studying how Twain prepped for his lectures. The site MDGAdvertising.com says Twain was "well ahead of his time in his ability to market his work while marketing himself as the definitive brand. He produced a steady stream of quality content and used laughter to drive loyalty. Though his heyday was more than 100 years ago, he still had the last word on modern marketing." Tom Bentley, writing for MarketingProfs.com says Twain "had 'platform' a century before the concept had circulation." (I don't know what "had 'platform'" means either.)

Twain scholar Laura Skandera Trombley has written thoughtfully about Twain as his own brand manager. She has noted how in 1909 the Mark Twain Company was no doubt the only company he was ever closely associated with that actually made money. With Rogers's help, Twain had already secured the copyrights to his own books. The purpose of the Mark Twain Company was to make it possible for him to generate income when other people wanted to use his likeness. Trombley writes:

> Once he copyrighted himself, he became an official commodity and possessed the right to control the usage of his likeness as well as the right to sue those who would use it without compensating him. An entire specialized area of business and copyright law has emerged from Mark Twain's efforts and celebrities like J Lo, Jessica Simpson, and Victoria Beckham should give him a grateful nod for creating the outlet that allows them to earn royalties from their clothing lines.

The estates of Elvis Presley, Michael Jackson, Marilyn Monroe, and other celebrities also owe Twain a debt of gratitude. Thanks to his pioneering efforts, heirs of celebrities today can generate huge revenues from the stars' images after their deaths —more, in some cases, than when they were alive.

WHEN TWAIN DIED in 1910, his estate was appraised at more than $470,000, or $11 million today. This included 50 shares in the Mark Twain Company worth $200,000, worth

$4.93 million now, and 375 shares of Plasmon Milk Products, which were worthless. In 1964, two years after his only surviving daughter, Clara, had died, his estate was worth just under $980,000, or about $7.6 million today. Her father's books continue to sell, of course. Some seem never to have been out of print. *Huckleberry Finn* makes his regular appearances in high school literature classes, though with equal regularity he is considered too disreputable for impressionable youth and expelled. He is always, of course, readmitted.

That Twain remains an immortal would no doubt please him greatly. Year after year, he still makes news of one kind or another, and when he does, sales of his books spike. He planned it that way, making sure of that by setting conditions on when his autobiography would be released. He began writing it in 1870, put it aside, then resumed work on it in 1906, this time dictating his memoirs. He allowed some cleaned-up excerpts to appear in the *North American Review* in 1906 and 1907 but was determined that the unexpurgated versions would not be released until well after he and everyone else he talked about (and sometimes denounced) in the memoirs were dead. Paine edited excerpts of the autobiography that appeared in 1924, followed by more extensive editions in 1940 and 1959. In 2010, the first of three volumes of his uncensored dictations was issued; the final volume was released in 2015. With each release there is a flurry of publicity, and once again we all talk about his books, chuckle over his spontaneous aphorisms, and wonder how his humor remains so fresh generation after generation.

So what lessons does this story of Twain's financial misadventures offer? What is the takeaway? What can we learn? Well, not much, probably. If you read this book in the hope that you would discover some secrets of financial success, you will no doubt put it down with a sense of disappointment, if not disgust. But that is the wrong way to read biographies and histories, anyway. The value in looking at the life and career of someone who lived at another time is not in search of cherry-picked anecdotes that illustrate some banality ("A good CEO is a good listener"). The value in reading biography and history is to expand one's imagination, to glimpse not how the challenges Twain faced were just like those of a business leader today (they weren't) but to learn how utterly different they were, and in that way enrich one's sense of life's complexity and even how wildly amusing the human condition really is. If that makes you a better businessperson, it would be because it has made you a better person, period—wiser, more understanding, and with a deeper sense of life's possibilities but also of its limitations.

Of course, we should remember that, as an investor, Twain lived in a world that did not really know about the business principles that we, a century later, take for granted. Investors in the late nineteenth century didn't have the same methods we have to conduct due diligence. They didn't always consult with lawyers when they drew up contracts. All too often, they relied on their gut impulses. What's puzzling, of course, is that a man who understood so much about human nature, as Twain did, could be misled so often by wishful thinking and a kind of manic enthusiasm.

Twain himself didn't believe there was much wisdom to be gained from a close examination of his business career. "I cannot say that I have turned out the great businessman that I thought I was when I began life," he told Eastern Business College alumni in Poughkeepsie in 1901, when he was sixty-five. "But I am comparatively young yet, and may learn." He then talked about Kaolotype ("I don't know now what it was all about"), and the Paige Compositor ("a machine for doing something or other"), and about how he failed even at book publishing, and reflected on how well served he had been through the years by his own mad and endless determination to make a great fortune.

Then, summing up his remarks to his business college audience, he offered one last thought for his listeners to hang on to.

"My axiom is," he said, after a long and impressive pause, "to succeed in business . . . avoid my example."

Afterword

And what about that Tennessee land that Twain's father said would make the family rich? In case you're wondering, John Marshall Clemens might have been right to tell his heirs to hang on to that property. The family had title to at least 30,000 acres, which John Clemens bought between 1826 and 1841, for $400 —or about $9,260 in our time.

Land records from Fentress County, where those land holdings were, show that in 2016, a parcel of 1,912 acres and the mineral rights under it sold for $2,453 per acre. That's a total of $4,690,136. So if Twain's family had kept those 30,000 acres to this day and sold them for $2,453 per acre, they'd have been worth at least $74 million. The family would have been "fabulously wealthy" after all.

Acknowledgments

I wish to thank Glen Hartley, my agent; Rick Wolff, my editor at Houghton Mifflin Harcourt; and Rick's superb publishing team, including Rosemary McGuinness, Alexandra Primiani, Dani Spencer, Katrina Kruse, Rachael DeShano, Lisa Sacks Warhol, Ayesha Mirza, and Martha Kennedy. They and their colleagues made the experience of writing this book a pleasure.

I am also grateful to Tom Gayner for his generosity and insight; to Steve Courtney at the Mark Twain House and Museum in Hartford for his expertise; to Kim Hasten, Gayle Kelly, and Robin Cheslock for their help with editing and research; to Mark Raper, Michael Whitlow, and Christian Munson, among others, who have been my gracious hosts at Padilla; and to Kent Masterson Brown, Stanley Craddock, Jane Glancy, Paul Hanks, Solomon Miles, and the late Kent Owen.

Much that I got right in this book is attributable to these people. If there are errors and I can think of anyone other than myself to blame for these lapses, their names will appear in later editions.

I owe special thanks, of course, to my beloved sons, Ned and Tim Crawford, and to my wife, Sally Curran, whose love, patience, and wisdom have made it possible for me to write books.

Notes

page

AUTHOR'S NOTE

x *"no ordinary genius"*: Samuel Charles Webster, *Mark Twain, Business Man* (Boston: Little, Brown, 1947), 140.
Twain "was a devil": Ibid., 277.

1. "WHATEVER I TOUCH TURNS TO GOLD"

3 *"part steamboat"*: Justin Kaplan, *Mr. Clemens and Mark Twain: A Biography* (New York: Simon & Schuster, 1966), 181.
"I increased the population": Charles Neider, ed., *Autobiography of Mark Twain* (New York: Harper & Row, 1959), 1.
4 *"The answer becomes obvious"*: Malcolm Gladwell, *Outliers: The Story of Success* (Boston: Little, Brown, 2008), 62.
"it really matters": Ibid.
5 *"The best time"*: Ibid., 63.
rightful Earl of Durham: Ron Powers, *Mark Twain: A Life* (New York: Free Press, 2005), 438.
"an over-surplus of property": Neider, *Autobiography*, 23.
"two or three Negroes": Ibid.
6 *"Money is better than poverty"*: Jon Winoker, *The Rich Are Different* (New York: Pantheon, 1996), 12.
"Whatever befalls me": Neider, *Autobiography*, 29.

"grazing lands": Ibid.

"the magnificent episode": John Maynard Keynes, *Critical Assessments: Second Series, Vol. 5*, ed. John Cunningham Wood (London: Routledge, 1994), 71.

7   *"the phenomenal release"*: George Wilson Pierson, *Tocqueville in America* (Baltimore: Johns Hopkins University Press, 1966), 770.

"the breathless generation": William Chamberlain, *The Enterprising Americans: A Business History of the United States* (New York: HarperCollins, 1974), 81.

"the continent lay": Elizabeth Stevenson, *Henry Adams: A Biography* (New York: Macmillan, 1997), 242.

"will henceforth increase": Neider, *Autobiography*, 29.

8   *"It's good to begin"*: Ibid., 32.

"inherited his father's aptitude": R. Kent Rasmussen, *Mark Twain A to Z: The Essential Reference to His Life and Writings* (New York: Oxford University Press, 1995), 81.

"my prescriptions were unlucky": Mark Twain, *Roughing It* (Mineola, NY: Dover, 2003), 151.

"customers bothered me": Ibid.

9   *"I am frightened"*: Albert Bigelow Paine, *Mark Twain: A Biography, Vol. II* (New York: Harper & Brothers, 1912), 821.

2. "THAT SPLENDID ENTERPRISE"

11   *"detested school"*: Albert Bigelow Paine, *Mark Twain: A Biography, Vol. I* (New York: Chelsea House, 1980), 69.

"I will promise": Ibid., 75.

12   *"hotbed of rest"*: Ron Powers, *Mark Twain: A Life* (New York: Free Press, 2005), 69.

"through the heart": Mark Twain, "The Turning Point of My Life," in *The Complete Essays of Mark Twain*, ed. Charles Neider (Garden City, NY: Doubleday, 1963), 480–81.

"coca enough to chew": William Lewis Herndon, *Exploration of the Valley of the Amazon: 1851–1852*, ed. Gary Kinder (New York: Grove Press, 2000), 47.

"It has made me": Ibid.

13   *"require no other sustenance"*: Powers, *Mark Twain*, 72.

14   *"at least to Moses"*: Leigh Buchanan, "How to Achieve Big Hairy Audacious Goals," *Inc.*, November 1, 2012, www.inc.com/leigh-bu chanan/big-ideas/jim-collins-big-hairy-audacious-goals.html.

"see their audacity": James C. Collins and Jerry I. Porras, *Built to Last: Successful Habits of Visionary Companies* (New York: HarperCollins, 1994), 104.

"*a longing to open up*": Twain, "Turning Point," 481.

"*agreed that no more*": Edgar Marquess Branch, Michael B. Frank, and Kenneth M. Sanderson, eds., *Mark Twain's Letters, Vol. 1, 1853–1866* (Berkeley: University of California Press, 1988), 66.

15 "*determined to start*": Ibid.

"*to take all the hell*": Ibid.

"*inquired about ships*": Harriet Elinor Smith, ed., *Autobiography of Mark Twain, Vol. 1* (Berkeley: University of California Press, 2010), 461.

16 "*A policeman came*": Mark Twain, *Essays and Sketches of Mark Twain* (New York: Sterling Publishing, 1995), 15.

"*that it would be difficult*": Paine, *Mark Twain, I,* 109.

"*This was all the thought*": Mark Twain, *Life on the Mississippi* (New York: Bantam, 1963), 25.

17 "*By temperament*": Twain, "Turning Point," 482.

3. "DO YOU GAMBLE?"

20 "*But I must smoke*": Albert Bigelow Paine, *Mark Twain: A Biography, Vol. I* (New York: Chelsea House: 1980), 118.

"*a private one*": Charles Neider, ed., *Autobiography of Mark Twain* (New York: Harper & Row, 1959), 57.

"*Very well*": Paine, *Mark Twain, I,* 119.

21 "*and the rest when I earn it*": Ibid.

22 "*When a circus came and went*": Mark Twain, *Life on the Mississippi* (New York: Bantam, 1963), 21.

"*the grandest position*": Ibid., 24.

23 "*an income equal*": Paine, *Mark Twain, I,* 145.

"*the largest boat*": Harriet Elinor Smith and Richard Bucci, eds., *Mark Twain's Letters, Vol. 2, 1867–1868* (Berkeley: University of California Press, 1990), 97.

"*to let the d—d rascals*": Edgar Marquess Branch, Michael B. Frank, and Kenneth M. Sanderson, eds., *Mark Twain's Letters, Vol. 1, 1853–1866* (Berkeley: University of California Press, 1988), 98.

"*moving mountains of light*": Ron Powers, *Mark Twain: A Life* (New York: Free Press, 2005), 77.

25 "*Good Lord, Almighty!*": David L. Levy, *Mark Twain: The Divided Mind of America's Best-Loved Writer* (Boston: Prentice Hall, 2011), 40.

4. "I HAD TO SEEK ANOTHER LIVELIHOOD"

27 "*the least sign*": Samuel Charles Webster, *Mark Twain, Business Man* (Boston: Little, Brown, 1947), 60.

28 *"incapacitated by fatigue"*: Charles Neider, ed., *Autobiography of Mark Twain* (New York: Harper & Row, 1959), 134.
   "learned more about retreating": David L. Levy, *Mark Twain: The Divided Mind of America's Best-Loved Writer* (Boston: Prentice Hall, 2011), 41.
   "I supposed": Ron Powers, *Mark Twain: A Life* (New York: Free Press, 2005), 256.
29 *"a not negligible position"*: Levy, *Mark Twain*, 44.
30 *"pure and fine"*: Mark Twain, *Roughing It* (Mineola, NY: Dover, 2003), 84.
31 *"was built to hold"*: Ibid.
   "galloping all over": Ibid.
   "It was wonderful": Ibid.
32 *"Within half an hour"*: Ibid.
   "Superb, Magnificent!": Edgar Marquess Branch, Michael B. Frank, and Kenneth M. Sanderson, eds., *Mark Twain's Letters, Vol. 1, 1853–1866* (Berkeley: University of California Press, 1988), 124.
   "the conflagration had traveled": Twain, *Roughing It*, 87.
33 *"looked like lava men"*: Branch, *Letters, 1*, 124.

5. "ALL THAT GLITTERS"

35 *"I would have been more"*: Mark Twain, *Roughing It* (Mineola, NY: Dover, 2003), 96.
   "literally bursting": Albert Bigelow Paine, *Mark Twain: A Biography, Vol. I* (New York: Chelsea House, 1980), 182.
36 *"was the road to fortune"*: Twain, *Roughing It*, 96.
   "is fabulously rich": Paine, *Mark Twain, I*, 175.
37 *"I confess"*: Twain, *Roughing It*, 103.
   "Think of it!": Ibid., 105.
   "All that glitters": Ibid.
38 *"it was found that"*: Ibid.
   "if we had towed the horses": Ibid.
39 *"One week of this"*: Ibid., 107.
   "So we went down": Ibid.
40 *"I think we had better"*: Samuel Charles Webster, *Mark Twain, Business Man* (Boston: Little, Brown, 1947), 17.
   "All too often": Charles Neider, ed., *Autobiography of Mark Twain* (New York: Harper & Row, 1959), 144.
   "had never grown": Twain, *Roughing It*, 131.
41 *"felt constrained to ask"*: Ibid.
   "I was discharged": Neider, *Autobiography*, 144.

"*It was not entirely*": Paine, *Mark Twain*, I, 199.

found "the real *secret*": Twain, *Roughing It,* 109.

42 "*bought and sold*": Ron Powers, *Mark Twain: A Life* (New York: Free Press, 2005), 108.

"We are rich!": Twain, *Roughing It,* 143.

6. "RICH AND BRIMFUL OF VANITY"

43 "*I thought the very earth*": Mark Twain, *Roughing It* (Mineola, NY: Dover, 2003), 143.

44 "*Let's—let's burn*": Ibid.

46 "*Hang the butcher!*": Ibid., 145–46.

"*managed to get it*": Ibid., 147.

47 "*busy with vain*": Ibid., 148.

"*I can always*": Ibid., 150.

"*the most curious*": Ibid., 141.

48 "*Send me $40*": Edgar Marquess Branch, Michael B. Frank, and Kenneth M. Sanderson, eds., *Mark Twain's Letters, Vol. 1, 1853–1866* (Berkeley: University of California Press, 1988), 189.

"*because I know*": Ibid., 105.

"*You have* promised": Ibid., 194–95.

49 "*until I am*": Ibid.

"*was avoiding acquaintances*": Twain, *Roughing It,* 229–30.

50 "*In the course*": Victor Fischer and Michael B. Frank, eds., *Mark Twain's Letters, Vol. 4, 1870–1871* (Berkeley: University of California Press, 1995), 148.

7. "THE RICHEST PLACE ON EARTH"

52 "*richest place on earth*": Warren Hinckle, *The Richest Place on Earth: The Story of Virginia City, Nevada, and the Heyday of the Comstock Lode* (Boston: Houghton Mifflin, 1978), vii.

"*I am very well satisfied*": Samuel Charles Webster, *Mark Twain, Business Man* (Boston: Little, Brown, 1947), 77.

"*Consequently, we generally*": Mark Twain, *Roughing It* (Mineola, NY: Dover, 2003), 159–60.

53 "*would squander half a column*": Ibid., 160.

"*washerwomen and servant girls*": Ibid., 159.

54 "*was Paradise to me*": Ibid., 224.

"*I attended private parties*": Ibid.

"*vested interest in euphoria*": John Kenneth Galbraith, *A Short History of Economic Euphoria* (New York: Penguin Business, 1994), 6.

"*The wreck was complete*": Twain, *Roughing It,* 225.

55 *"spasms of virtue"*: Charles Neider, ed., *Autobiography of Mark Twain* (New York: Harper & Row, 1959), 139.
"Once more, native imbecility": Twain, *Roughing It*, 228.
56 *"the town fell into decay"*: Ibid., 233.

8. "POOR, PITIFUL BUSINESS!"

57 *"a little book"*: Louis J. Budd, ed., *Mark Twain: The Contemporary Reviews* (Cambridge: Cambridge University Press, 1999), 28.
"I don't believe": Albert Bigelow Paine, *Mark Twain: A Biography, Vol. I* (New York: Chelsea House, 1980), 320.
58 *"utterly miserable"*: Edgar Marquess Branch, Michael B. Frank, and Kenneth M. Sanderson, eds., *Mark Twain's Letters, Vol. 1, 1853–1866* (Berkeley: University of California Press, 1988), 322.
"I have had a 'call'": Ibid.
59 *"The temperance virtue"*: Charles Neider, ed., *Autobiography of Mark Twain* (New York: Harper & Row, 1959), 287–88.
"never entirely forgive": Samuel Charles Webster, *Mark Twain, Business Man* (Boston: Little, Brown, 1947), 87–88.
60 *"Doors open at 7 o'clock"*: Paine, *Mark Twain, I*, 292.
"quaint, apparently unconcerned": "Mark Twain on Artemus Ward," *Brooklyn Daily Union*, November 22, 1871.
61 *"could not help"*: Mark Twain, *The Innocents Abroad* (New York: Harper & Brothers, 1911), 162.
"We are perhaps": Paine, *Mark Twain, I*, 350.
"the best business judgment": Ibid., 157.
"is always good-humored humor": William Dean Howells, *My Mark Twain: Reminiscences and Criticisms*, ed. Marilyn Austin Baldwin (Baton Rouge: Louisiana State University, 1967), 89.
62 *"full of point and pungency"*: Budd, *Mark Twain*, 82.
"I am not married": Resa Willis, *Mark and Livy: The Love Story of Mark Twain and the Woman Who Almost Tamed Him* (New York: Atheneum, 1992), 33–34.
"I want a good wife": Ibid.

9. "IT IS OURS — ALL OURS — EVERYTHING"

63 *"I'll harass that girl"*: Resa Willis, *Mark and Livy: The Love Story of Mark Twain and the Woman Who Almost Tamed Him* (New York: Atheneum, 1992), 41.
64 *"Huge chandeliers"*: Ibid., 37.
"character, in case": Charles Neider, ed., *Autobiography of Mark Twain* (New York: Harper & Row, 1959), 247.

"frank to a fault": Harriet Elinor Smith, ed., *Autobiography of Mark Twain, Vol. 1* (Berkeley: University of California Press, 2010), 226.

65 *"would fill a drunkard's grave"*: Willis, *Mark and Livy*, 40.
"I'll be your friend": Ibid., 248.
"unconsciously cheat": Smith, *Autobiography*, 1, 471.

66 *"People who can afford"*: Albert Bigelow Paine, *Mark Twain: A Biography, Vol. I* (New York: Chelsea House, 1980), 394.
"put us into a boarding-house": Neider, *Autobiography*, 156.
"Mr. Langdon": Paine, *Mark Twain, I*, 396.

10. "IN FAIRYLAND"

67 *"Little Sammy"*: Ron Powers, *Mark Twain: A Life* (New York: Free Press, 2005), 283.
"most credulous": John Kenneth Galbraith, *A Short History of Economic Euphoria* (New York: Penguin Business, 1994), 6.
"the pet scheme": Victor Fischer and Michael B. Frank, eds., *Mark Twain's Letters, Vol. 4, 1870–1871* (Berkeley: University of California Press, 1995), 258–60.

68 "dead sure tricks": Ibid.
"sound as a drum": Fischer, *Letters*, 4, 262–63.

69 *"just as if"*: Ibid., 251.
"will be packing his trunk": Ibid.
"for one hundred thousand dollars": Ibid., 331.
"Let the diamond fever": Justin Kaplan, *Mr. Clemens and Mark Twain: A Biography* (New York: Simon & Schuster, 1966), 127.

70 *"pumped dry"*: Ibid., 128.
"a kind of technological grandeur": Ibid., 126.

71 *"anti-sun-stroke hat"*: Powers, *Mark Twain*, 300.
"An inventor is a poet": Samuel Charles Webster, *Mark Twain, Business Man* (Boston: Little, Brown, 1947), 114.
"modest little drilling machine": Ibid.

72 *"could have made"*: Harriet Elinor Smith, ed., *Autobiography of Mark Twain, Vol. 1* (Berkeley: University of California Press, 2010), 145.
"the most extraordinary": Fischer, *Letters*, 4, 465.

73 *"While I dressed"*: Ibid., 463.

74 *"While the literature claims"*: Rebecca Greenfield, "Celebrity Invention: Mark Twain's Elastic Clasp Brassiere Strap," *The Atlantic*, July 1, 2011, www.theatlantic.com/technology/archive/2011/07/celebrity-invention-mark-twains-elastic-clasp-brassiere-strap/241267/.
"We should refocus": Ibid.

75 *"Taking full advantage"*: Fred Kaplan, *The Singular Mark Twain: A Biography* (New York: Doubleday, 2003), 256.

11. "TO LIVE IN THIS STYLE . . ."

77 *"Hartford dollars have a place"*: Kenneth R. Andrews, *Nook Farm: Mark Twain's Hartford Circle* (Cambridge, MA: Harvard University Press, 1950), 18.

78 *"To live in this style"*: Ibid., 19.
"one of the best of men": Peter Messent, *Mark Twain and Male Friendship: The Twichell, Howells, and Rogers Friendships* (New York: Oxford University Press, 2009), 50.
"castigated [his congregants for]": Andrews, *Nook Farm*, 15–16.
"fetch a whoop": Ibid., 88.

79 *"build it right"*: Ibid., 24.
"The carpenters are here": Michael B. Frank and Harriet Elinor Smith, eds., *Mark Twain's Letters, Vol. 6, 1874–1875* (Berkeley: University of California Press, 2002), 247.
"even if we": Steve Courtney, *"The Loveliest Home That Ever Was": The Story of the Mark Twain House in Hartford* (Mineola, NY: Dover, 2011), 106.
"oddest-looking buildings": Ibid.
"brick-kiln gone crazy": Ibid.
"This Italy": Resa Willis, *Mark and Livy: The Love Story of Mark Twain and the Woman Who Almost Tamed Him* (New York: Atheneum, 1992), 122.

80 *"still had a little cash"*: Carole Thomas Harnsberger, *Mark Twain at Your Fingertips: A Book of Quotations* (Mineola, NY: Dover, 2009), 360.
"Why, they've even": Albert Bigelow Paine, *Mark Twain: A Biography, Vol. II* (New York: Harper & Brothers, 1912), 572.
"take off that ugly roof": Courtney, *"The Loveliest Home,"* 127.

81 *"whole-souled hosts"*: Willis, *Mark and Livy*, 96.
"never plain": Courtney, *"The Loveliest Home,"* 50.
"It is octagonal": Milton Meltzer, *Mark Twain Himself* (New York: Bonanza, 1960), 146.

82 *"Canadian pirates"*: Paine, *Mark Twain, II*, 686.
"he shan't run": Victor Fischer and Michael B. Frank, eds., *Mark Twain's Letters, Vol. 4, 1870–1871,* (Berkeley: University of California Press, 1995), 127.
"did not contain": Paine, *Mark Twain, II*, 457.

83 *"gum-stickum, to ward off"*: Ron Powers, *Mark Twain: A Life* (New York: Free Press, 2005), 324.

"you need not wet": Albert Bigelow Paine, ed. *Mark Twain's Letters* (New York: Harper & Brothers, 1917), 196.

"ought to be good evidence": Ibid.

"malleable as a spaniel": Powers, *Mark Twain,* 324.

"splendid, immoral, tobacco-smoking": Gregg Camfield, *The Oxford Companion to Mark Twain* (New York: Oxford University Press, 2003), 556.

"the unholiest gang": Albert Bigelow Paine, *Mark Twain: A Biography, Vol. I* (New York: Chelsea House, 1980), 352.

"as a solemn fast-day": Harriet Elinor Smith and Richard Bucci, eds., *Mark Twain's Letters, Vol. 2, 1867–1868* (Berkeley: University of California Press, 1990), 57.

84 *"As security"*: Charles Neider, ed., *Autobiography of Mark Twain* (New York: Harper & Row, 1959), 303.

12. "HOW THE IGNORANT AND INEXPERIENCED SUCCEED"

85 *"Mr. Samuel L. Clemens"*: Michael B. Frank and Harriet Elinor Smith, eds., *Mark Twain's Letters, Vol. 6, 1874–1875* (Berkeley: University of California Press, 2002), 668.

86 *"big-hearted man"*: Benjamin Griffin and Harriet Elinor Smith, eds., *Autobiography of Mark Twain, Vol. 2* (Berkeley: University of California Press, 2010), 56.

"Certainly there is": Peter Krass, *Ignorance, Confidence, and Filthy Rich Friends: The Business Adventures of Mark Twain, Chronic Speculator and Entrepreneur* (Hoboken, NJ: John Wiley, 2007), 95–96.

87 *"an institution"*: Ibid.

"went to pieces": Frank, *Letters,* 6, 171.

"a line of artificial": Ibid., 55–56.

88 *"waiting for Jones"*: Ibid.

"There are not many": Ibid.

"was prepared to seek": Charles Neider, ed., *Autobiography of Mark Twain* (New York: Harper & Row, 1959), 305.

"He believed": Ibid.

89 *"The device"*: Deborah Smith Pegues and Ricky Temple, *Why Smart People Make Dumb Choices* (Eugene, OR: Harvest House, 1982), 158.

"was driving around": Neider, *Autobiography,* 305.

"the first one": Ibid.

90 *"like adding a hundred servants"*: Resa Willis, *Mark and Livy: The*

Love Story of Mark Twain and the Woman Who Almost Tamed Him (New York: Atheneum, 1992), 139.

"profanity-breeding": Carole Thomas Harnsberger, *Mark Twain at Your Fingertips: A Book of Quotations* (Mineola, NY: Dover, 2009), 469.

"It is my heart-warm": Ibid.

13. "A LIE & A FRAUD"

92 *"I can get along"*: Harriet Elinor Smith and Richard Bucci, eds., *Mark Twain's Letters, Vol. 2, 1867–1868* (Berkeley: University of California Press, 1990), 254.

"an engine or a furnace": Charles Neider, ed., *Autobiography of Mark Twain* (New York: Harper & Row, 1959), 301.

"He was a specialist": Ibid.

"on a salary": Ibid., 302.

93 *"the other dollar"*: Ibid.

"The steam pulley": Ibid.

94 *"We've quit being poor"*: Resa Willis, *Mark and Livy: The Love Story of Mark Twain and the Woman Who Almost Tamed Him* (New York: Atheneum, 1992), 120.

"suggested that I reserve it": Ibid., 127.

95 *"I am so sorry"*: Harriet Elinor Smith, ed., *Autobiography of Mark Twain, Vol. 1* (Berkeley: University of California Press, 2010), 471.

to Titian: Hamlin Hill, ed., *Mark Twain's Letters to His Publishers, 1867–1894* (Berkeley: University of California Press, 1967), 117.

"the best process": Ibid., 116.

"will utterly annihilate": Samuel Charles Webster, *Mark Twain, Business Man* (Boston: Little, Brown, 1947), 142.

96 *"increase the value"*: Ibid., 148.

97 *"I never saw people"*: Ibid.

"If the utility": Ibid.

"for wall-paper stamps": Ibid.

98 *"who seemed"*: Benjamin Griffin and Harriet Elinor Smith, eds., *Autobiography of Mark Twain, Vol. 2* (Berkeley: University of California Press, 2010), 54.

complete authority: Fred Kaplan, *The Singular Mark Twain: A Biography* (New York: Doubleday, 2003), 364.

"were to be": Webster, *Mark Twain, Business Man*, 154.

99 *"the case is"*: Ibid.

"took advantage": Peter Krass, *Ignorance, Confidence, and Filthy Rich Friends: The Business Adventures of Mark Twain, Chronic Speculator and Entrepreneur* (Hoboken, NJ: John Wiley, 2007), 113.

"be proceeded against": Ibid., 112.

"The bubble has burst": Frederick Anderson, Lin Salamo, and Bernard L. Stein, eds., *Mark Twain's Notebooks & Journals, Vol. II (1877–1883)* (Berkeley: University of California Press, 1975), 393.

100   *"stole from me"*: Griffin, *Autobiography*, 2, 490.

"That raven flew out": Ibid., 54.

"to a man": Ibid.

"I have some good news": Henry Nash Smith, ed., *Mark Twain–Howells Letters: The Correspondence of Samuel L. Clemens and William D. Howells, 1872–1910* (Cambridge: Belknap Press, 1960), 236.

101   *"that hated property"*: Smith, *Autobiography*, 1, 471.

14. "THE PROPORTIONS OF MY PROSPERITY"

103   *"insults, for two months"*: Resa Willis, *Mark and Livy: The Love Story of Mark Twain and the Woman Who Almost Tamed Him* (New York: Atheneum, 1992), 139.

"Charley, do you": Samuel Charles Webster, *Mark Twain, Business Man* (Boston: Little, Brown, 1947), 358.

104   *"ten years of swindlings"*: Benjamin Griffin and Harriet Elinor Smith, eds., *Autobiography of Mark Twain, Vol. 2* (Berkeley: University of California Press, 2010), 52.

"skinny, yellow, toothless": Harriet Elinor Smith, ed., *Autobiography of Mark Twain, Vol. 1* (Berkeley: University of California Press, 2010), 241.

"nothing about subscription": Griffin, *Autobiography*, 2, 53.

105   *"even Noah got"*: Ibid., 58.

"something entirely new": Ibid.

"starting life": Ibid.

"to complain about": Ron Powers, *Mark Twain: A Life* (New York: Free Press, 2005), 482.

106   *"No one seems"*: Webster, *Mark Twain, Business Man*, 279.

"greater than literature": Ibid., 218.

"thought of nothing else": Ibid.

"If you haven't": Albert Bigelow Paine, ed., *Mark Twain's Letters* (New York: Harper & Brothers, 1917), 436.

107   *"I think that"*: Webster, *Mark Twain, Business Man*, 221–23.

"looked like a cross": Peter Krass, *Ignorance, Confidence, and Filthy Rich Friends: The Business Adventures of Mark Twain, Chronic Speculator and Entrepreneur* (Hoboken, NJ: John Wiley, 2007), 99.

"put it aside": Hamlin Hill, ed., *Mark Twain's Letters to His Publishers, 1867–1894* (Berkeley: University of California Press, 1967), 307.

108 *"invented a more expensive"*: Webster, *Mark Twain, Business Man,* 279.

"*You haven't asked*": Robert Pack Browning, Michael B. Frank, and Lin Salamo, eds., *Mark Twain's Notebooks & Journals, Vol. III (1883–1891)* (Berkeley: University of California Press, 1979), 74.

109 *"Try again"*: Webster, *Mark Twain, Business Man,* 291.

"*I was used*": Ibid., 266.

"*I might have*": Ibid., 297.

"*Some people*": Ibid., 279.

110 *"heave your surplus energies"*: Ibid., 267.

"put in ten or twelve thousand": Benjamin Griffin and Harriet Elinor Smith, eds., *Autobiography of Mark Twain, Vol. 3* (Berkeley: University of California Press, 2015), 332.

"had a number": Albert Bigelow Paine, *Mark Twain: A Biography, Vol. III* (New York: Chelsea House, 1980), 1151.

111 *"an early example"*: "Not on Mark Twain's Watch," *Robb Report,* August 1, 2007, http://robbreport.com/watches/editors-not-mark-twains-watch.

"He would remember me": Albert Bigelow Paine, *Mark Twain: A Biography, Vol. II* (New York: Harper & Brothers, 1912), 652.

112 *"sweeping out the offices"*: Griffin, *Autobiography,* 2, 61.

"commercial magnitude": Albert Bigelow Paine, *Mark Twain: A Biography, Vol. II* (New York: Harper & Brothers, 1912), 800.

"General, if that": Ibid.

"General," he went on: Ibid., 801.

113 *"given us"*: Paine, *Letters,* 452.

114 *"totally free from debt"*: Ibid., 467.

"frightened by the proportions": Webster, *Mark Twain, Business Man,* 301.

15. "THIS AWFUL MECHANICAL MIRACLE"

115 *"which was my study"*: Albert Bigelow Paine, *Mark Twain: A Biography, Vol. II* (New York: Harper & Brothers, 1912), 903.

116 *"I knew all about"*: Ibid., 903–4.

"always taking little chances": Harriet Elinor Smith, ed., *Autobiography of Mark Twain, Vol. 1* (Berkeley: University of California Press, 2010), 101.

"bright-eyed, alert": Paine, *Mark Twain, II,* 904.

117 what it *"now costs"*: Robert Pack Browning, Michael B. Frank, and Lin Salamo, eds., *Mark Twain's Notebooks & Journals, Vol. III (1883–1891)* (Berkeley: University of California Press, 1979), 424.

"does not get drunk": Ibid., 147.

"*10 will* get *work*": Ibid., 437.

118 "*It is thus*": Frederic Bastiat, *The Bastiat Collection* (Auburn, AL: Ludwig Von Mises Institute, 2007), 34.

119 "*What will it cost?*": Smith, *Autobiography, 1,* 104.
"*can bankrupt you*": Paine, *Mark Twain, II,* 906.
"*began to calculate*": Ibid.

120 "*It takes a thousand*": Albert Bigelow Paine, ed., *Mark Twain's Letters* (New York: Harper & Brothers, 1917), 731–32.

121 "*inside of twelve months*": Browning, *Notebooks & Journals, III,* 215.
"*all ready to talk*": Ibid.

122 "*The machine is*": Albert Bigelow Paine, *Mark Twain: A Biography,* Vol. III (New York: Chelsea House, 1980), 907–8.
"*to have unlimited*": Resa Willis, *Mark and Livy: The Love Story of Mark Twain and the Woman Who Almost Tamed Him* (New York: Atheneum, 1992), 173.
"*I expect to write*": Ron Powers, *Mark Twain: A Life* (New York: Free Press, 2005), 515.

123 "*What a talker*": Paine, *Mark Twain, II,* 965.

124 "EUREKA!": Ibid., 908.
"*This is by far*": Ibid.
"*All the other*": Ibid.

16. "OUR PROSPERITY BECAME EMBARRASSING"

126 "*in a sort of delirious*": William Dean Howells, *My Mark Twain: Reminiscences and Criticisms,* ed. Marilyn Austin Baldwin (Baton Rouge: Louisiana State University, 1967), 61–62.
"*a couple of pounds*": Samuel Charles Webster, *Mark Twain, Business Man* (Boston: Little, Brown, 1947), 361.

127 "*would cost nearer*": Ibid.
"*You did well*": Ibid., 364.
"*Ah," she said*: Resa Willis, *Mark and Livy: The Love Story of Mark Twain and the Woman Who Almost Tamed Him* (New York: Atheneum, 1992), 170.

128 "*coat of bleu stuff*": Webster, *Mark Twain, Business Man,* 388.
"*We were very short*": Ibid.
"*are nearer my size*": Ibid., 364.
"*stir in this household*": Ibid., 261.

129 "*to send some money*": Ibid., 367.
"*The Greatest Book*": Justin Kaplan, *Mr. Clemens and Mark Twain: A Biography* (New York: Simon & Schuster, 1966), 289.
"*going to go*": Webster, *Mark Twain, Business Man,* 377.

"We did not consider": Howells, *My Mark Twain*, 62.

130   *"had decided that"*: Albert Bigelow Paine, *Mark Twain: A Biography*, Vol. II (New York: Harper & Brothers, 1912).

"sanguine soul": Kaplan, *Mr. Clemens*, 290.

"what we call menial work": Andrew Gyory, *Closing the Gate: Race, Politics, and the Chinese Exclusion Act* (Chapel Hill: University of North Carolina Press, 2000) 248–49.

131   *"I do not love"*: Robert Pack Browning, Michael B. Frank, and Lin Salamo, eds., *Mark Twain's Notebooks & Journals, Vol. III (1883–1891)* (Berkeley: University of California Press, 1979), 272.

132   *"Beecher," it was said*: Barry Werth, *Banquet at Delmonico's* (New York: Random House, 2009), 20.

"If he writes": Ron Powers, *Mark Twain: A Life* (New York: Free Press, 2005), 514.

"a chance to play": Benjamin Griffin and Harriet Elinor Smith, eds., *Autobiography of Mark Twain, Vol. 2* (Berkeley: University of California Press, 2010), 74.

"to pass some marked": Ibid., 73.

133   *"color went out"*: Ibid., 75.

"the finest suburb": Browning, *Notebooks & Journals, III*, 323.

134   *"It was easy"*: Griffin, *Autobiography, 2*, 75.

"War literature of any kind": Browning, *Notebooks & Journals, III*, 430.

"Probably everybody": Webster, *Mark Twain, Business Man*, 387.

135   *"Father of Ovariotomy"*: Powers, *Mark Twain*, 536.

"infinitely grander & finer": Hamlin Hill, ed., *Mark Twain's Letters to His Publishers, 1867–1894* (Berkeley: University of California Press, 1967), 245.

"Customers had to pay": Richard Zacks, *Chasing the Last Laugh: Mark Twain's Raucous and Redemptive Round-the-World Comedy Tour* (New York: Doubleday, 2016), 7–8.

136   *"The faster installment"*: Ibid., 8.

"I am not whining": Browning, *Notebooks & Journals, III*, 375.

"the slightest thing": Webster, *Mark Twain, Business Man*, 386.

"How long he has been": Browning, *Notebooks & Journals, III*, 374.

137   *"an exceedingly hard summer"*: Webster, *Mark Twain, Business Man*, 386.

"an attack of grip": Columbus (GA) *Enquirer*, April 29, 1891, 1.

"Publisher of Gen. Grant's Memoirs": Browning, *Notebooks & Journals, III*, 625.

"want him to drop it": Webster, *Mark Twain, Business Man*, 391.

"You and I": Browning, *Notebooks & Journals, III*, 395.

17. "GET ME OUT OF BUSINESS!"

139 *"I tell [Livy] that"*: Albert Bigelow Paine, *Mark Twain: A Biography*, Vol. II (New York: Harper & Brothers, 1912), 961.

140 *"keep the ship afloat"*: Ibid.
"Mrs. Clemens says": Ibid., 962.
"hoped to sell": Robert Pack Browning, Michael B. Frank, and Lin Salamo, eds., *Mark Twain's Notebooks & Journals*, Vol. III (1883–1891) (Berkeley: University of California Press, 1979), 574.

141 *"about the same length"*: Ibid., 640.
"I have a vote": Ibid., 574
"the Paradise of the Rheumatics": Ibid., 623.
"the disease world's bathhouse": Harriet Elinor Smith, ed., *Autobiography of Mark Twain*, Vol. 1 (Berkeley: University of California Press, 2010), 74.

142 *"private feed"*: Ibid., 456.
"making a joyful": Ibid.
"that baby": Samuel Charles Webster, *Mark Twain, Business Man* (Boston: Little, Brown, 1947), 396.

143 *"beyond description"*: Albert Bigelow Paine, *Mark Twain: A Biography*, Vol. III (New York: Harper & Brothers, 1912), 965.
"is superb, it is perfect": Browning, *Notebooks & Journals*, III, 573.

144 *"It does not seem credible"*: Paine, *Mark Twain*, II, 965.
"That's a mistake": Ibid., 964.

145 *"a most daring and majestic liar"*: Fred Kaplan, *The Singular Mark Twain: A Biography* (New York: Doubleday, 2003), 472.
"The bloody machine": Paine, *Mark Twain*, II, 967.
"Paige and I": Richard Zacks, *Chasing the Last Laugh: Mark Twain's Raucous and Redemptive Round-the-World Comedy Tour* (New York: Doubleday, 2016), 6.

146 *"flirting with a good-looking clerk"*: Corban Goble, "Mark Twain's Nemesis: The Paige Compositor," a paper presented at the Annual Meeting of the Association for Education in Journalism and Mass Communications, August 3–6, 1985.
"We are skimming along": Kaplan, *The Singular Mark Twain*, 473.
"unless we sell": Ibid., 441.

147 *"I am terribly tired"*: Paine, *Mark Twain*, II, 966.

18. "HIS MONEY IS TAINTED"

149 *"drank almost a whole bottle"*: Lewis Leary, ed., *Mark Twain's Correspondence with Henry Huttleston Rogers, 1893–1909* (Berkeley: University of California Press, 1969), 10.

150 *"if they go"*: Albert Bigelow Paine, *Mark Twain: A Biography, Vol. II* (New York: Harper & Brothers, 1912), 968.
"Nothing," he said: Leary, *Correspondence with H. H. Rogers*, 114.
"telling her": Ron Powers, *Mark Twain: A Life* (New York: Free Press, 2005), 554.
"raced around Wall Street": Leary, *Correspondence with H. H. Rogers*, 11.

151 *"so physically exhausted"*: Peter Krass, *Ignorance, Confidence, and Filthy Rich Friends: The Business Adventures of Mark Twain, Chronic Speculator and Entrepreneur* (Hoboken, NJ: John Wiley, 2007), 190.
"had ventured": Leary, *Correspondence with H. H. Rogers*, 11.
"I want you": Paine, *Mark Twain, II*, 970.

152 *"an irascible and contemptuous"*: Leary, *Correspondence with H. H. Rogers*, 3.

153 *"as fine a pirate"*: Ibid., 5.
"giant trust": Ibid., 4–5.
"grinding up the poor": Ibid., 7.
"was of that class": Ibid., 8.
"the Artful Dodger": Richard Zacks, *Chasing the Last Laugh: Mark Twain's Raucous and Redemptive Round-the-World Comedy Tour* (New York: Doubleday, 2016), 25.
"It's a pity": Powers, *Mark Twain*, 562.

19. "MARK TWAIN LOSES ALL"

156 *"men who were there"*: Lewis Leary, ed., *Mark Twain's Correspondence with Henry Huttleston Rogers, 1893–1909* (Berkeley: University of California Press, 1969), 4.
"serene, patient": Albert Bigelow Paine, *Mark Twain: A Biography, Vol. III* (New York: Chelsea House, 1980), 1659.
"time is worth": Benjamin Griffin and Harriet Elinor Smith, eds., *Autobiography of Mark Twain, Vol. 2* (Berkeley: University of California Press, 2010), 161.
"The only man": Benjamin Griffin and Harriet Elinor Smith, eds., *Autobiography of Mark Twain, Vol. 3* (Berkeley: University of California Press, 2015), 231.
"stop walking": Albert Bigelow Paine, ed., *Mark Twain's Letters* (New York: Harper & Brothers, 1917), 596.

157 *"better than a circus"*: Leary, *Correspondence with H. H. Rogers*, 17.

158 *"to hang this last"*: Ibid., 19.
"bankrupt, deep in debt": Richard Zacks, *Chasing the Last Laugh:*

Mark Twain's Raucous and Redemptive Round-the-World Comedy Tour (New York: Doubleday, 2016), 19.

"is the only one": Ibid.

"I came up": Leary, *Correspondence with H. H. Rogers,* 20.

"Farewell—a long farewell": Ibid., 20.

161 *"a classic hedge"*: Zacks, *Chasing the Last Laugh,* 23–24.

"devouring every pound": Albert Bigelow Paine, *Mark Twain: A Biography, Vol. II* (New York: Harper & Brothers, 1912), 984.

"Failure of Mark Twain,": Zacks, *Chasing the Last Laugh,* 28.

"It is another": Ibid., 29.

162 *"my second is to those others"*: Ibid., 31.

"It was confoundedly difficult": Ibid., 32.

20. "KNOCKED FLAT ON MY BACK"

163 *"will come and want"*: Lewis Leary, ed., *Mark Twain's Correspondence with Henry Huttleston Rogers, 1893–1909* (Berkeley: University of California Press, 1969), 83.

"it cannot make": Ibid., 89.

"got knocked flat": Ibid., 95–96.

164 *"that would have been* foresight*"*: Ibid., 98.

"stand by for a cyclone!": Ibid., 99–100.

165 *"at as low"*: Ibid., 104.

"an absolutely sure": Ibid., 107.

"spent two francs": Ibid., 100.

"knocked every rag": Ibid., 108.

166 *"I must be there"*: Ibid.

"with just barely": Ibid., 109.

"diphthongs, fractions": Ibid., 110.

"was a marvelous invention": Albert Bigelow Paine, *Mark Twain: A Biography, Vol. III* (New York: Chelsea House, 1980), 991.

167 *"though it would"*: Richard Zacks, *Chasing the Last Laugh: Mark Twain's Raucous and Redemptive Round-the-World Comedy Tour* (New York: Doubleday, 2016), 44.

"If we can rent": Leary, *Correspondence with H. H. Rogers,* 118.

"is to teach myself": Ibid., 118–19.

"To that": Ibid., 119.

168 *"I never had a friend"*: Ibid., 112.

"Every day": Ibid., 4.

169 *"Why ask Rogers?"*: Ibid., 7.

"take a breath": Zacks, *Chasing the Last Laugh,* 45.

21. "MONEY FOR A MONUMENT"

171 *"bondage of debt"*: Resa Willis, *Mark and Livy: The Love Story of Mark Twain and the Woman Who Almost Tamed Him* (New York: Atheneum, 1992), 232.

"acres of figures": Kenneth R. Andrews, *Nook Farm: Mark Twain's Hartford Circle* (Cambridge: Harvard University Press, 1950), 231.

172 *"I guess I am"*: Albert Bigelow Paine, *Mark Twain: A Biography, Vol. I* (New York: Chelsea House, 1980), 409–10.

"I hope your business troubles": Richard Zacks, *Chasing the Last Laugh: Mark Twain's Raucous and Redemptive Round-the-World Comedy Tour* (New York: Doubleday, 2016), 30.

"This time": Willis, *Mark and Livy*, 225.

"lectured and robbed": Albert Bigelow Paine, *Mark Twain: A Biography, Vol. II* (New York: Harper & Brothers, 1912), 79.

"after which": Willis, *Mark and Livy*, 225.

173 *"constant unceasing adulation"*: Ibid., 218.

"I am sure": Ibid., 220.

"What had started": Zacks, *Chasing the Last Laugh*, 161.

174 *"I appreciate"*: Lewis Leary, ed., *Mark Twain's Correspondence with Henry Huttleston Rogers, 1893–1909* (Berkeley: University of California Press, 1969), 306.

"For the first time": Ibid., 310.

"I hope you": Albert Bigelow Paine, *Mark Twain: A Biography, Vol. III* (New York: Chelsea House, 1980), 1055–56.

175 *"retire gracefully"*: Leary, *Correspondence with H. H. Rogers*, 283.

"This way out": Ibid., 284.

176 *"I wish you would"*: Ibid., 286.

"a second American embassy": Willis, *Mark and Livy*, 248.

177 calls fraudulent: Zacks, *Chasing the Last Laugh*, 23–24.

"as one of the first": "The Hero as Man of Letters," *New York Times*, October 30, 1900.

"It is as an American": Ibid.

22. "YOU CANNOT LOSE A PENNY"

179 *"renewed youth"*: Resa Willis, *Mark and Livy: The Love Story of Mark Twain and the Woman Who Almost Tamed Him* (New York: Atheneum, 1992), 257.

"Among us": Lewis Leary, ed., *Mark Twain's Correspondence with Henry Huttleston Rogers, 1893–1909* (Berkeley: University of California Press, 1969), 445.

180 *"pure albumin"*: Ibid., 505.
"*acted like poisons*": Ibid.
"*implored them all*": Ibid., 506.
"*Yes—take it as medicine*": Albert Bigelow Paine, *Mark Twain: A Biography, Vol. III* (New York: Chelsea House, 1980), 1151.
181 "*The scientific testimonials*": Fred Kaplan, *The Singular Mark Twain: A Biography* (New York: Doubleday, 2003), 576.
"*feed the world's hungry*": Willis, *Mark and Livy*, 254.
"*automatically punches*": Leary, *Correspondence with H. H. Rogers*, 337.
"*merely expecting*": Richard Zacks, *Chasing the Last Laugh: Mark Twain's Raucous and Redemptive Round-the-World Comedy Tour* (New York: Doubleday, 2016), 365.
182 "*could get my living*": Leary, *Correspondence with H. H. Rogers*, 328.
"*I've landed*": Ibid., 327.
"*Competition would be*": Ibid., 338.
183 "*I do not feel*": Peter Krass, *Ignorance, Confidence, and Filthy Rich Friends: The Business Adventures of Mark Twain, Chronic Speculator and Entrepreneur* (Hoboken, NJ: John Wiley, 2007), 226.
"*or with wool*": Leary, *Correspondence with H. H. Rogers*, 343.
"*was about time*": Ibid., 436.
"*It's as good as*": Ibid., 445.
184 "*five or six fingers*": Zacks, *Chasing the Last Laugh*, 382–83.
"*would consider*": Leary, *Correspondence with H. H. Rogers*, 560.
185 "*Mark Twain is*": "Receiver Wants to See Mark Twain," *New York Times*, January 30, 1908.
"*It is*": Gary Scharnhorst, ed., *Mark Twain: The Complete Interviews* (Tuscaloosa: University of Alabama Press, 2006), 660.
"*If I had kept out*": Leary, *Correspondence with H. H. Rogers*, 561.
"*Do be careful*": Kaplan, *The Singular Mark Twain*, 595.

23. "TO SUCCEED IN BUSINESS . . ."

187 "*broken down*": Richard Zacks, *Chasing the Last Laugh: Mark Twain's Raucous and Redemptive Round-the-World Comedy Tour* (New York: Doubleday, 2016), 342.
"*If Mark Twain*": Ibid., 343.
188 "*The report of my illness*": Ibid.
190 "*well ahead of his time*": "8 Branding Tactics Marketers Can Learn From Literary Legend Mark Twain," *Advertising and Marketing Blog*, MDG Advertising, September 27, 2013, www.mdgadvertising .com/blog/8-branding-tactics-marketers-can-learn-from-literary -legend-mark-twain/.

191 *"had 'platform'"*: Tom Bentley, "Mark Twain's 10-Sentence Course on Branding and Marketing," MarketingProfs, July 15, 2013, www .marketingprofs.com/articles/2013/11152/mark-twains-10-sentence -course-on-branding-and-marketing.

"Once he copyrighted himself": Laura Skandera Trombley, "America's First Modern Celebrity," *The Daily Beast*, March 20, 2010, www.thedailybeast.com/articles/2010/03/20/americas-first-modern -celebrity.html.

193 *"I cannot say"*: *Mark Twain's Speeches* (New York: Harper & Brothers, 1910), 341.

194 *"My axiom is"*: Ibid.

Index

About the Author

Alan Pell Crawford is the author of *Twilight at Monticello: The Final Years of Thomas Jefferson, Unwise Passions: The True Story of a Remarkable Woman and the First Great Scandal of Eighteenth-Century America,* and *Thunder on the Right: The "New Right" and the Politics of Resentment.* His articles have appeared in the *Wall Street Journal,* the *New York Times,* and the *Washington Post.*

Formerly a resident scholar at George Washington's Mount Vernon and at the International Center for Jefferson Studies at Monticello, Crawford has spoken at Harvard University, the Cooper Union in New York, the Union League Club of New York City, and the U.S. Department of the Treasury's Executive Institute, among others.

Crawford lives in Richmond, Virginia, with his wife, Sally Curran, an editor at the Virginia Museum of Fine Arts. They have two grown sons, Ned and Tim.

Crawford's band, the Ham Biscuits, is available for both public and private events.

He can be reached at Alanpellcrawford@gmail.com.